MASTERING
KARATE

Jerry Beasley

Human Kinetics

Library of Congress Cataloging-in-Publication Data

Beasley, Jerry, 1950-
  Mastering karate / Jerry Beasley.
    p. cm
  Includes index.
   ISBN: 0-7360-4410-8 (soft cover)
  1. Karate I. Title.
   GV1114 .3 .B44 2003
   796.815'3--dc21

                                                                2002009246

ISBN: 0-7360-4410-8

Acquisitions Editor: Edward McNeely
Developmental Editor: Cynthia McEntire
Managing Editors: Anne Cole, Kim Thoren
Copyeditor: John Wentworth
Proofreader: Pam Johnson
Indexer: Craig Brown
Permission Manager: Toni Harte
Graphic Designer: Robert Reuther
Graphic Artist: Francine Hamerski
Photo Manager: Dan Wendt
Cover Designer: Kristin Darling
Photographer (cover): Jack Jeffers
Photographer (interior): Lora Gordon, unless otherwise noted. Photos on pages 22, 23, 24, 26, 27, 29, 30, 45, 46, 80, 89, 96, 119, and 140 by Larry Ritchie; photos on pages 32, 37, 41, 145, 155, and 156 by Ric Anderton; photos on pages 146 and 147 by Century Martial Arts; photos on page 47 by Patrick Purdue; photo on page 142 by Bob Caldwell; photo on page 144 by Kathy Gillis; photo on page 164 by Gina Beasley; photo on page 87 by Jack Jeffers.
Printer: United Graphics

Human Kinetics books are available at special discounts for bulk purchase. Special editions or book excerpts can also be created to specification. For details, contact the Special Sales Manager at Human Kinetics.

Printed in the United States of America   10 9 8 7 6 5 4 3 2 1

Human Kinetics
Web site: www.HumanKinetics.com

United States: Human Kinetics
P.O. Box 5076
Champaign, IL 61825-5076
800-747-4457
e-mail: humank@hkusa.com

Canada: Human Kinetics
475 Devonshire Road Unit 100
Windsor, ON N8Y 2L5
800-465-7301 (in Canada only)
e-mail: orders@hkcanada.com

Europe: Human Kinetics
107 Bradford Road
Stanningley
Leeds LS28 6AT, United Kingdom
+44 (0) 113 255 5665
e-mail: hk@hkeurope.com

Australia: Human Kinetics
57A Price Avenue
Lower Mitcham, South Australia 5062
08 8277 1555
e-mail: liahka@senet.com.au

New Zealand: Human Kinetics
P.O. Box 105-231, Auckland Central
09-523-3462
e-mail: hkp@ihug.co.nz

A seeker of truth once approached a wise man and asked, "Teacher, what master do you honor?" The wise man responded, "The One who is the same yesterday, today, and forever. It is He who forgives the past and gives the future." "How, then, may I honor Him?" asked the seeker. The teacher replied, "When you do honor to the least of men you honor Him. He is worthy."

Peace.

CONTENTS

FOREWORD

Dr. Jerry Beasley, a nationally known sports sociologist, university professor, practitioner, competitor, and teacher of Asian martial arts for the last 35 years, has written a well-researched and comprehensive book. *Mastering Karate* clearly and precisely discusses the history, sociology, evolution, and development of karate, from the classical Japanese system of Funakoshi, founder of Shotokan in the 1930s, to the modern American system of karate practiced today in the United States. Beasley defines the updated American karate system as "a mixing of skills and practice methods . . . eclectic, non-classical, freestyle, and independent."

The author supports the view of famed movie star Bruce Lee, founder of Jeet Kune Do (JKD), that traditional martial arts is "not unlike a tomb that restricts self-expression" and in which "the classical karateka become so immersed in following 'the way' that they develop dependent minds incapable of anything but imitation." Beasley advocates liberation from the limitations imposed by classical karate. He champions the cause of freedom in transcending the control and restriction of one system by incorporating, integrating, cross-training, blending, and mixing the best techniques of several well-known Asian martial arts, thus developing the most effective American style of fighting.

The Beasley Matrix for Martial Arts provides a unique and novel way of evaluating various systems, including karate, judo, jiujitsu, hapkido, kickboxing, taekwondo, kung fu, and aikido. The matrix is a systematic method in examining the most salient components of different styles. It is a revolutionary way of testing, comparing, assessing, and teaching the effectiveness of various defensive and offensive techniques.

Mastering Karate is highly methodical, well-structured, and easy to read for both beginners and seasoned martial artists. It is well illustrated with photos of outstanding martial artists such as Joe Lewis, Chuck Norris, Bruce Lee, Bill Wallace, Jeff Smith, and many others. Photos of Dr. Beasley and his partners provide step-by-step demonstration from classical to modern combative techniques covering stances, blocking, kicking, striking, trapping, kneeing, tripping, sweeping, and many other techniques. This book also covers important subject such as nonclassical self-defense techniques, strategies for competition, and innovative teaching and training methods for modern American karate.

Mastering Karate represents freedom to express martial skills without limitation. Mastering karate means mastering the self. "We have gained mastery when we are free to express all views," says Beasley. He has skillfully presented the creative, eclectic, and integrative development of modern American karate. This book is a must for all serious karate practitioners.

M. Gyi, PhD
Professor Emeritus, Ohio University
Chief Instructor, American Bando Association

PREFACE

To many, the word *karate* evokes the image of a young man fighting an imaginary enemy on a sandy beach. A red sunset in the background sends glimmering golden light beams dancing across the ocean waves. The man wears a traditional karate gi, his belt moving rhythmically at his waist as he moves through the kata of his style. His knuckles, somewhat callused, reveal the passion of his focus.

Like so many before him, he might have entered the discipline for self-defense. Beating up the school bully is a fantasy that never seems to subside. However, after countless battles in the dojo—battles that have become symbolic of life and death—he at last seeks only peace, the absence of conflict.

When confronted by an aggressor, he is free to turn the other cheek. He has used karate, translated as "the empty hand," to empty his mind of fear. As the karateka, he has engaged in symbolic violence within the community that has become the dojo.

Now he will avoid an encounter, for he knows only too well the dangers of unleashing the force of his empty hands. It is this power that so many originally come to karate to attain, yet when it is fully possessed it is cast aside. At this point karate has become a way of life.

I am pleased to have been asked to author this book on mastering karate. I first learned of the art of karate from the neighborhood bully. We all were afraid of him, and that's why we were drawn to him.

His name was Roy, and he would tell us stories about war and fighting. The only story I still remember was how Paladin, the hero of a 1950s western television series who was a fast-gun soldier of fortune and carried a card that read "Have gun, will travel," had defeated several bad guys using karate.

The year was probably 1960 when I first learned of karate. To a nine-year-old boy, having such power as could be found in karate was quite inviting. With no other information available about this enchanting martial art, I eventually became more interested in hunting, fishing, camping, and exploring the woods, fields, and streams near my Southwest Virginia home.

By the fall of 1965, things had changed. That was the year when Robert Conrad starred as James West in the *Wild, Wild West* television series. James West was a James Bond–style secret agent, trained in the martial arts. Each Friday night I was glued to the television screen, dreaming of learning karate.

I ordered the Charles Atlas and Joe Weider courses in "Devastating Kung Fu and Jiujitsu," but I learned very little. In 1966, I bought a copy of Mas Oyama's *What is Karate?* and practiced in secret in the mountains, just like Oyama. Then in 1968, a Korean karate instructor opened a school near my home.

The instructor was Whit Davis, and he helped introduce me to the way of karate. Since 1968, I have been either a student or instructor of the way of karate. I have been fortunate to have studied with some excellent instructors, including masters Lee, Kim, and Kang, who taught me taekwondo and hapkido. I learned boxing from Maynard Quesenberry and kali from Dan Inosanto. I practiced judo with Olympian Jerry Shedd and kodokan judo with Dr. Fred Waddell. Master Chin was my primary instructor for kung fu and tai chi, and Joe Lewis taught me the most about American karate and kickboxing.

I've been influenced by the styles of many of the instructors I've worked with over the years. Michael DePasquale, Sr., Wally Jay, Fumio Demura, Chuck Norris, Bill Wallace, and Renzo Gracie have all served as role models for me in the martial arts. I have also spent many years redacting the philosophy of jeet kune do presented by Bruce Lee.

To further my knowledge of martial arts, I earned college degrees in philosophy, sociology, and education. Each time I was assigned a paper or project, I somehow managed to focus on Eastern philosophy, status in the dojo, role expectations, or martial arts curriculum design. Some of the information included in this book was excerpted from my research that led to a master's thesis and doctoral dissertation at Virginia Tech.

I hope that the reader will understand that karate is a way, or *do*. The physical skills have always varied from one instructor to another. Whether your interpretation of karate is Japanese, Okinawan, American, Chinese, Korean, Brazilian, Filipino, or Indonesian makes little difference. The titles and classifications we provide serve only to establish our own limitations.

If in my style of karate I must perform my side kick one way, and in your style of karate you are limited to performing your way, what have we accomplished? We have established conflict based on prejudice, ethnocentrism, and perhaps intolerance. These characteristics limit the advancement of true karate-do.

Mastering karate means mastering the self. We have gained mastery when we are free to express all views. Bruce Lee, in attempting to define the concept of freedom of expression, called the process jeet kune do. We can just as easily call it karate. In this book, mastery is defined as freedom. Thus, as we master karate we gain freedom to express any skills without limitation.

ACKNOWLEDGMENTS

First, I would like to thank my wife, Gina, for her editorial assistance in transforming my handwritten paper into a completed manuscript. Thanks also to the folks at Human Kinetics, especially Ed McNeely, who recruited me for the project, and Kim Thoren, who was willing to consider my points of view.

Special thanks to the lead photographer, Lora Gordon, and to Jack Jeffers, who shot the cover photo. Thanks also to Ric Anderton and Larry Ritchie who supplied many of the historical and celebrity photos.

Finally, thanks is extended to the models: James Houston, Ian Marshall, Eric Eberhardt, Larry Carter, and Gina Beasley. And, of course, to the superstars of modern karate who have helped shape the development of American karate including Joe Lewis, Chuck Norris, Bill Wallace, and the many champions whose images appear on the pages of this book and in the memories of thousands of karateka.

INTRODUCTION

Men grind and grind in the mill of a truism, and nothing comes out but what was put in. But the moment they desert the tradition for a spontaneous thought, then poetry, wit, hope, virtue, learning, anecdote, all flock to their aid.

—Ralph Waldo Emerson

Through research I have found that, historically, the social structure and philosophy of any given art has been equally as important as the selection of physical skills contained within the art. The fortification of an art's physical potential should always be considered a positive course of development. Moreover, the progressive adoption of a multicultural perspective serves to substantially improve the utility of the art. Such is the case in the art and sport of modern karate.

Although the history and traditions of karate date back several centuries, the art was virtually nonexistent in the United States prior to the mid-1950s. From its introduction on the West Coast to its sustained popularity nationwide, the practice of karate has attracted millions of people to this once typically Oriental martial art. So varied were the martial arts styles brought to this country (by Asian masters seeking economic opportunities and World War II veterans returning home with new methods of hand-to-hand fighting) that American practitioners were able to pick and choose among the traditional arts for elements that best matched their personal tastes and goals.

The variety of techniques in karate afforded the astute martial artist the opportunity to combine the skills and training procedures of different styles. The mixing and integration of skills created a form of karate that was uniquely American. As if sparked by a cultural tradition of assimilating opposing views for the common good, Americans over the past 60 years have formulated a recognizable contemporary form of karate. As practiced in the United States today, karate represents an eclectic improvement of physical skills and martial philosophy representing the most successful of the Oriental arts originally taught in this country.

The term *karate* (pronounced kah-rah-tay) is comprised of two Chinese characters: *kara*, which translates as "empty," and *te*, which means "hand" or "fist." An often repeated oral history suggests that during its early development karate was practiced in secret by an oppressed Okinawan society forbidden to possess weapons. Thus, the practice of karate served as a means to prepare the body for combat. The body became the weapon—each foot a sword, each arm a spear, each hand a knife. In addition to using the arms, legs, and fists, the karateka developed the *kiai* (pronounced kee-I), a meeting of the body and mind (or spirit), which accompanied each potentially deadly blow.

While the word *karate* originated in the Chinese language, the term has been similarly adopted into the Japanese language and finds common usage in Okinawa. *Karate* is also a popular term in the United States, as well as in the rest of the world. However, the use of the word *karate* may result in different interpretations among various groups. The evolution of karate has caused the word itself to acquire many definitions. For example, in the United States the term *karate* might signify a particular Japanese art or be used as a generic term for fighting arts.

To add to the complexities of using the term there are several different forms of karate, each employing a particular method and philosophy. Some of the forms represent their enveloping countries, so the use of different terminology reflecting national origins is quite common. For example, Chinese karate is sometimes referred to as *wu shu* or the popular term *kung fu*. Japanese and Okinawan martial arts more often are called *karate*, and Korean arts are known as *tang soo do* or *taekwondo*. Each national form of martial art might also be represented by several distinct styles. For example, Japanese and Okinawan karate may be called *goju ryu*, *shotokan*, *shito ryu*, or *isshin ryu*. A style might be further distinguished as Chinese *goju* or Okinawan *isshin ryu*. The Korean karate called *taekwondo*, introduced to this country in the 1960s, is very different from the Korean *taekwondo* of the 1980s and 1990s.

When addressing practitioners of a particular style, proper etiquette suggests that we refer to each art by the name that denotes that particular style of the art. Often, certain groups identify with a particular name that tends to separate their art from other karate styles. Since some prestigious styles have gained notice through the physical prowess of their exponents, identification with such styles often entitles the practitioner to a certain amount of respect from other *karateka* (karate enthusiast or student) of lesser styles.

In many cases, the effects of pronounced style identity result in conflicting views among opposing martial arts factions. This conflict has caused many contemporary writers and martial artists to denounce the emphasis on maintaining a separation of groups through style identity. With a trend toward mixing styles both in street defense and in tournament competition, the significance of individual styles has greatly depreciated. To be competitive with modern-day sport fighters, you have to learn the specifics of both tournament-style karate and mixed martial arts. Consequently, many traditional styles have been updated to allow for "Americanized" sparring skills. Karate instructors who focus their instruction on self-defense have learned to incorporate realistic skills and training methods from sources outside classical styles.

As martial arts have adapted to contemporary practices, the use of traditional Asian terminology has in many cases been abandoned and the English equivalent substituted. However, certain words introduced via martial arts practitioners have found continuous use and are now widely accepted in karate groups. Terms such as *sensei*, which means "honorable teacher"; *dojo*, which means "training hall" or "school"; and *gi*, or "uniform," are commonly used in reference to Oriental fighting arts.

For our purposes here, we'll use the term *karate* to address equally the arts of karate and some interpretations of kung fu and taekwondo as sharing characteristically similar historical development in the United States. To be sure, Americans generally refer to punching and kicking arts (whether they are, in fact, more like taekwondo or kung fu) as karate.

In many contemporary karate classes, traditional skills are combined with grappling, boxing, and weapons arts to form functional self-defense methods. You need not feel obliged to maintain a particular style, as doing so serves little function—rather, you're free to use whatever techniques prove effective. Thus, the term *karate* is also employed to denote those martial arts systems that include a mixing of styles and are readily adaptable to change.

The emphasis on pageantry and ritual expressed by many traditional practitioners is often a primary concern. This emphasis on tradition (doing things because they always have been done) tends to relegate utility in combat, the goal of martial arts, to a lesser position. Without combat efficiency, any martial art is reduced.

It's quite acceptable to practice an art with the sole objective of artistic expression and character development. However, you should be aware of the primary concern of the art form. Contemporary nonclassical karate stresses combat efficiency, even if it means adapting skills from many arts. The goal of karate continues to be to prepare a person for combat in the shortest amount of time. As times have changed, karate instructors typically have adapted to the expectations of their clientele, thus supplementing the physical skills employed in their arts. Other changes have included using music during training, wearing full body armor to better simulate combat drills, and introducing new belt colors, gi styles, and training attire. Additionally, new rules have been developed to govern the methods of kumite.

Experience has taught us that the single most significant characteristic of any martial art is the social structure incorporated by its followers. This social structure—the way people relate to each other—when changed will have more effects on students than the simple addition or deletion of physical techniques. It would be an endless discussion, for example, to argue the merits of incorporating an isshin ryu vertical punch over the taekwondo turnover punch. In similar context, it makes little difference whether a hand strike based on an animal form (often used in kung fu, a forerunner of karate) is more valid than a similar strike in another art that deletes the animal analogy. However, when we attempt to change the social structure of the class (delete the bow, remove the rank system, and so on), the art begins to deteriorate. What remains is simply a group of physical exercises.

In the final analysis, the physical skills of karate and karate-like arts (kung fu and taekwondo) have always varied. That which bonds these arts together is the social structure, the chain of command, and the feeling of being a part of something that has withstood the test of time.

Chapter 1 introduces you to an ultra-traditional social structure still practiced in some karate schools. In most modern schools, only a general structure is maintained, as we have found that too much tradition confines development. Such development, or changing of physical and social skills, was at one time thought to be a dishonorable trait. While physical skill might be equally developed through alternate means, the social skills of respect, discipline, and allegiance to a leader are perhaps more noticeably developed through the traditional military structure discussed in chapter 1.

The Roots of Contemporary Karate

Several years ago, as a graduate research student, I conducted an interpretive analysis of the social interaction component to the process of socialization into the techniques and ideology of karate. The data was obtained through participant observation; use of informants, periodicals and testimonials; interviewing; activity analysis; and an extensive survey. The data was collected between the years 1973 and 1977. I include the information from that analysis in this text because I believe that any thorough analysis of karate must explore karate training within a context of social meaning at both an idealized and functional level. Successful karate instructors address both the acquisition of physical skills and the social dimensions that will result in success or failure for the dojo.

In my research I found that it is important that the student in the karate dojo earn membership in a peer group (associated with rank) and that this membership facilitate the student's advancement to the next level. Moreover, each new level must redefine the student's sense of purpose and feeling of self-worth, commitment to the cause, and valued membership in the group. Because the majority of karate students will never test their skills in street encounters, true karate teaches one to avoid hurting others, even if that means turning the other cheek to the aggressor. The effectiveness of the art is measured in everyday interaction with others, both in the dojo and in public.

An art that can address the social needs of a diverse group can grow to include many loyal devotees. The way we teach the art is more important than what techniques are defined as part of our art. Thus, karate (including Japanese, Korean, American, and Chinese interpretations) has been the most successful form of self-defense ever developed.

Many come to karate to learn self-defense and, in so doing, gain confidence, respect, a feeling of self-worth, and other enviable traits. Ask any karate instructor what he or she teaches, and almost always the instructor will mention the students' acquisition of these characteristics as part of the overall program. Most schools incorporate sophisticated physical self-defense techniques with diverse patterns for instilling these highly regarded character traits.

Karate is a regimented leisure activity. Therefore, each participant undergoes a socialization process in which he or she takes on the values of the group, with the focus of achieving the behavioral goals important to the group. Karate participants engage in a challenging program in which they are asked to submit to the requirements of a dangerous activity. Instructors teach self-defense skill by carefully leading students through exercises. In the process, students come to recognize the importance of acquiring these skills and, by internalizing the values of the group, tend to refrain from using their skills in all but the most threatening situations.

The development of the right attitude is as important as the acquisition of self-defense skills. Therefore, instructors need to spend as much time outlining a plan to accomplish character development as they do in teaching self-defense skills. With minimum effort, an instructor can acquire an effective method for providing the other part of instruction—the right attitude. The outline acts as a rite of passage system in which the student will be at ease in the proper setting (the *dojo*), recognize the values of the group (etiquette), learn the skills of self-defense in the class routine, and demonstrate his ability to others (promotion).

This chapter outlines the socialization process used in traditional karate schools and discerns the manner in which the right attitude can develop in the process of learning self-defense. The right attitude may be exemplified in a person's willingness to help others and walk away from a fight, honesty, courage, and other traits mentioned in the Code of Bushido, the Samurai code of conduct on the battlefield, commonly recognized by all karate styles.

THE TRADITIONAL DOJO

The traditional, or classical, dojo was first introduced in the United States in the mid-1950s. Now, these traditional schools are being replaced with more contemporary dojos that lack the militaristic posture once thought necessary for success. Many of the great masters were brought up in the traditional dojo setting. However, a majority of today's karate students have little knowledge of the origins of the karate dojo. It remains to be seen whether modern dojos that lack the traditional social structure can educate students with the same level of social conformity valued by traditionalists.

The Japanese term *dojo* is given to the training hall in which the physical techniques and cultural traditions of karate are taught. The grand patriarch of the dojo is the *sensei*, who as teacher and chief role model sets the example for students to follow. Because of the camaraderie and group identity enhanced by the dojo, it is sometimes seen as a pseudo-family unit in which students are referred to as brothers and the sensei regarded as the father.

The status structure of the dojo is divided into a clearly defined social hierarchy based on skill attainment and dramaturgical adeptness, or a person's ability to act the part. As the student progresses from novice to black belt, ideally he comes to accept a disciplined way of sport and life reflected in the cultural traditions, pageantry, and rituals of karate that are integral to the social fabric of the dojo.

Bushido, Black Belts, and Broken Boards

Although they are often considered uniquely Oriental, karate, kung fu, and other Asian fighting arts bear some semblance to ancient Western combative methods. A form of shadow boxing that Plato called "fighting without an antagonist" uses an imaginary opponent, which is strikingly similar to *kata*, or form training, a method of practicing karate. The popular method of breaking inanimate objects characteristic of karate training was demonstrated well over 2,000 years ago by Greek and Roman boxers who broke stones for spectator appeal. Additionally, the *karateka*'s (karate enthusiast's) emphasis on abdominal shouting (called *kiai*, or spirit meeting) was used by ancient Greeks and others who used empty hand or primitive weapon-oriented arts.

Though we may conclude that, historically, all fighting skills exhibit some physical similarities, we also may note that each skill exhibits the culture of its enveloping society. For this reason, we may say that Chinese boxing differs from Roman boxing because Chinese boxing emphasizes spiritual development, a reflection of cultural values.

In most cases, the development of physical prowess is a primary goal of learning fighting skills. With the development and acceptance of modern weaponry, hand-to-hand combat became less effective for any situation. However, certain fighting skills were valued more for their cultural and intellectual expression than for their effectiveness in war. Indeed, some societies maintained their fighting arts for the sake of promoting social skills exemplified in the pageantry and ritual of the martial art. For example, the knights of feudal England aligned their fighting skills with a code of ethics called *chivalry*. Chivalry as a moral code found expression in what was known as rules of fair play in fighting; it gained acceptance as the commonly reinforced expectations of performance. In short, the precepts of knighthood—the practice of courtesy, respect, loyalty, and so on—were characteristic of the social ideals of the society.

As the need for the knights' specialized fighting skills disappeared, the corresponding moral code also lost its appeal, because the actualization of chivalry required physical abilities acquired only through success in battle. In times of peace, when the battlefield was no longer the meeting place for warriors, tournaments were popular. Regardless of whether the battle was real or make-believe, the physical success of victory and the resulting self-confidence permitted the actualization of chivalry and in turn were tempered by it.

Just as the knights maintained a code of ethics exemplified in their martial skills, Japanese samurai also were noted for conduct in battle. Samurai, known primarily for their martial arts skills, gained popularity in Japan during the Muromachi period (1392-1573), when the Japanese warlords gained prominence.

The bushi, or samurai, were employed by the warlords to protect their lands. To best serve their lords' purpose, the samurai developed *bugei*, martial arts that used both empty hand and weapons combat. A samurai's daring deeds and displays of tenacity in personal combat immortalized his fighting skills and his loyalty to a master. The samurai was a professional fighter because he was paid a salary and given other benefits.

Though he dealt in violence and death, the samurai was a man of honor who swore undying allegiance to his master. *Bushido*, the way of the warrior, was the ethical and philosophical code of the samurai. Bushido was a moral standard composed of justice, courage, benevolence, politeness, veracity, honor, and loyalty that determined the use of the samurai's skills. The samurai was at once both a brutally efficient killer who lacked Western conscience and a culturally gentle and civilized man by the standard of the day.

The samurai was expected to study martial arts with the sole intention of attaining self-perfection. Martial arts taught physical skills and mental development; these two were not to be separated. The samurai did not seek mental perfection without seeking physical perfection, or physical perfection without seeking the other.

Originally samurai used martial fighting skills to protect the group cause. Martial arts training developed the right frame of mind and technical skills for defending or promoting the warlord's cause. During times of feudal war, the bushi could test his martial prowess and practice bushido in his daily affairs.

As feudal warlords became obsolete, the fighting samurai became less a part of society. The samurai found that his martial arts training was no longer a necessity. The martial arts that were once a way of life for the samurai were now confined to practice in the dojo. In the dojo, the practitioner could engage in mock battle in the form of sportlike competition and actualize the precepts of bushido.

As martial arts moved from the battlefield to the dojo, the practitioners carried with them the pageantry and ritual, cultural norms, and traditional values that had governed their mode of behavior for centuries. Thus the dojo became a place in which people could assume new roles replete with symbolic status and maintain the virtues of 17th-century Japanese knighthood, even in 21st-century United States.

Feng Shui in the Dojo

Feng shui is the structural ecology and cultural decor in the dojo. The popularity of karate made the dojo a ubiquitous establishment on the American urban scene and precipitated a diffusion of bushido and Oriental martial arts that involve individuals from all walks of life. Given the large number of people who pursue karate and other martial arts, it is interesting that an apparent alternate status universe, a way of recognizing and conforming different groups into a homogenous classroom, ultimately takes shape in each dojo. This society of karateka is reinforced (indeed, formed) in part by the efficient design of the dojo.

The classical dojo. Students are led through rigorous kata. There is little room for individuality in a class that stresses obedience and conformity. Many of the great champions of American karate learned the art in a classical dojo.

For devotees, the dojo is more than a space. The dojo is designed to facilitate a unique way of life in which a feeling of brotherhood and love for the dojo is developed. Traditionally, each student was responsible for the upkeep of the dojo. Class might begin with all students—doctors, lawyers, and janitors alike—on their knees wiping down the hallowed halls of the dojo.

These and other experiences in humility served to form both a union of mind and body and a sense of belonging in which a student recognized and accepted the importance of his position in the life of the group. A well-arranged and decorated dojo sets the stage for a student to accept the instruction and forget his life outside the dojo.

In general, the dojo tries to create an atmosphere in which the student can become properly indoctrinated in Oriental culture and ideology as part of socialization in the martial arts. This socialization emphasizes achieving an effective dramaturgical context to lend credence to the dojo. The structuring of the various areas serves to use space and decor to alter mood and elicit appropriate behaviors. In effect, the ecology and decor of the dojo aim to satisfy customers' desire to assume an ephemeral and exotic social role: It provides a dramaturgical context with the trappings of Oriental culture, and it restructures operations through a functional separation of dojo space.

A dojo might include an office area in which certificates or awards are displayed. Seeing the certificates and trophies awarded to the dojo, the student enters the dojo through the office. In some dojos, the office serves as a general store in which karate items are marketed and sold. Guests and parents are required to stay in the waiting room or viewing area so that practitioners (especially young karateka) are separated from family and friends, permitting the sensei to exercise more complete control over instruction and indoctrination. In some dojos, viewing areas are not permitted.

The teaching area usually includes mirrors or other teaching aids and appropriate decorations suggesting the school's style, former masters, and the like. The workout area is usually arranged so that students face national flags when they enter the area. In most cases, mirrors, punching bags, and weight training equipment are found in the workout area. A larger dojo may have changing areas (including dressing rooms, showers, and lockers) separate from other facilities.

The traditional dojo is decorated with calligraphy composed of characters that correspond to the appropriate language and other items from the country represented. For example, a Korean karate dojo would have the Korean flag, statues representing Korean art, and perhaps a few pictures of famous Korean karate masters on the wall. Likewise, a Japanese dojo would exhibit Japanese art and calligraphy to associate the student or visitor with Japanese cultural traditions.

Dojo Etiquette

The karate student's behavior in the dojo is prompted by deep respect for the practice hall, its purpose, and the people who use it. All students are expected to adhere to a precisely circumscribed code of conduct from the moment they enter the dojo until they leave the premises. Dojo etiquette is a

Karate begins and ends with respect for one's opponent.
Here, the author demonstrates the traditional bow (*a-b*) and ready position (*c-d*).

ceremonial form adopted from the martial customs of the Orient and is rigidly observed by the practitioners of most Asian fighting arts today.

Upon entering the dojo, the student bows to the practice area in the direction of the national flags. If a sensei is present before class begins, students bow to the sensei and exchange words of appreciation. The manner of the bow varies with the martial art. Basically, the student begins to bow by standing erect and then bending at the waist, hands by the sides. He then resumes an erect position. Certain styles of karate, however, may require that the student strike the chest with the hands as he bends forward, perform a particular hand movement, or recite a series of phrases declaring his allegiance to his art and its country of origin.

Because karate is a vigorous activity, students are expected to wear clean uniforms and shower before and after workouts. During the practice session, talking usually is forbidden as is chewing gum or making inappropriate noises. Before leaving the mat, students bow to the sensei, then to the flags, and once again to the dojo as they leave. While bowing or talking to the sensei, the student is expected not to stare the sensei in the eye (or to make any eye contact) because this may be considered a demonstration of insincerity.

THE STATUS SYSTEM

Status ranking in the karate dojo is a reflection of the national habits and customs of its enveloping society. For example, Asian society places an emphasis on the superior–subordinate relationship, and in such relationships a person tends to assume the position that corresponds to his particular status level within the society. Thus, the karate neophyte is thrust into a position of subservience and must accept the attendant posture of humility and deference to superiors until he may be able to elevate himself through demonstration of progressive levels of proficiency in the sport.

The system also provides each person with an indication of his position in relation to others within the group. Martial artists and experts in Japanese culture reinforce the attitude that the martial arts status ranking system is a reflection of the junior/senior structure seen at all levels in Japan.

In essence, each member loses a sense of individuality by maintaining an allegiance to the organizational structure. It has been said that the Japanese maintain a denial of individualism in favor of a collective orientation. The collective orientation is an indication to some that group membership is considerably more important to the Japanese than to Americans.

In pre–World War II Japanese society, the system gave each person his own niche and permitted him to experience security and purpose within the group. Furthermore, the organizational structure made the individual feel a degree of responsibility to the group (he accepts their values, adheres to group norms, and so on). Thus the individual subsequently supports the system that included him in its order.

This philosophy of putting the group ahead of self may seem strange in western culture. In fact, at the end of World War II, many Americans were shocked to learn that so many Japanese had committed ritualized suicide in response to losing the war. So strong was the shared sense of responsibility that some Japanese felt that the only way to save face was to give their lives as testimony of shared remorse.

One of the more interesting social dimensions of the hierarchical structure seen in the practice of karate concerns the availability of achieved status. A person can move rapidly through the hierarchy and attain clearly defined status, a fact that no doubt appeals to the social mobility-conscientious American. In this regard, modern-day martial arts dojos are somewhat similar to fraternal organizations in which one enters the system in a subordinate position and, through experience and demonstrated proficiency, assumes positions of increasingly higher status and social honor. The status associated with acquired skill allows practitioners to enjoy a higher degree of prestige and recognition regardless of their social position outside the organization.

One sociological study found that most advanced students in some inner-city dojos of the 1970s tended to be working-class males. The researchers observed that through the social order of the belts the advanced students could realize the respect and success that otherwise would not be available to them in society. The karate dojo offers an attractive status arena for members of the working class because they can achieve meaningful recognition through the symbolic social mobility of the hierarchical proficiency structure of the sport.

Today, some 30 years later, it is more likely that the status system available in the dojo attracts those from all strata of society. College students in particular seem to enjoy the rank system, as do professionals in all lines of work. Today a majority of karate students are children who are encouraged by their parents to advance in rank. These parents may well experience advancement vicariously through the achievements of their children.

Although all martial arts ranks maintain certain similarities (they begin with white and progress to black, for example), some segments of the martial arts sports may promote students in a manner unique to a given discipline. Students in the dojo are divided into two categories: kyu rank (or grade) and dan rank (or degree). The kyu (Japanese), gup (Korean), or grade rank refers to beginners. Dan (Japanese), dun (Korean), or degree ranks are awarded to advanced students. It has been asserted that one is considered a true student of karate only when he has attained the rank of first-degree black belt.

As the student progresses through the grades from 10 through 1, corresponding belt colors give the student additional recognition. Belt colors usually are awarded in the order for the grades shown in table 1.1. In some cases the dojo may award a red belt instead of a brown one or an orange belt instead of a gold one, for example. Because instructors charge for promotion, some instructors use additional colored belts as part of the cost of promotion. Korean karate practitioners use a red belt instead of a brown belt in most cases. In addition to the colors, students may wear hashmarks that designate their grades in the color. For example, a green belt may have one

TABLE 1.1	
Grade	**Belt color**
10 to 9	White to yellow
8 to 7	Gold, yellow, or orange
6 to 4	Green or blue
3 to 1	Brown or red

mark designating the rank of fifth grade or two marks designating fourth grade. As students demonstrate advanced skills, they may be tested for higher ranks.

Hypothetically, students may advance, be demoted, or receive no change at all at each testing period. Students are encouraged to test for advancement because higher rank carries increased prestige and authority in the dojo. Whereas white belts are considered babies and relegated to standing in the back of the class, higher grades such as brown belt or student black belts assume positions at the head of the class next to the sensei. Full progression in the pecking order develops as the student advances from the back of the lines (white belt), to the center lines (green belt), to the front lines (brown belt), perhaps eventually to the head of the class upon acquiring the position of instructor or sensei. Examinations are given every three months. A student usually is ready to test for a higher grade rank at each promotion.

Advancing in rank is important to the student because advanced students receive more attention from the sensei, and advanced rank entitles the student to participation in advanced instructional periods. These privileges are sociologically important as they facilitate the acquisition of skills that in turn may elevate the person's position even more.

CLASS ROUTINE

Competition for advancement in karate is expected, with each student attempting to learn as much as possible during instructional periods to minimize his chances of failure at the next testing period. For the karate student, each series of class routines trains him for the next level of proficiency.

As he rises in rank, he learns the skills associated with the subsequent status and prepares to advance to a new rank at the end of the three-month period. The student follows a cycle in development—earn rank, adjust to the position, test and assume a new rank, adjust, test, and so on.

Before, during, and after each class routine, the student takes part in a learning process that eventually will complete his integration of dojo technique and ideology and assure his full acceptance into the group. The cycle of development parallels an effective socialization process in which the individual develops a social self that corresponds to the generalized other characterizing the group.

As the student enters the dojo, he bows before entering the workout area and then changes clothes. The practice uniform, or *gi*, consists of loose-fitting pants, a wrap-around jacket, and a belt. Because karate training facilitates fitness and requires that the student be physically fit, some students take time and pleasure in changing clothes so as to give full exposure to their well-developed bodies. Students exhibiting outstanding muscular development receive recognition from both fellow students and sensei.

In the traditional dojo, women are treated the same way as men in both sparring and physical training. In this regard, the dojo seems to emphasize a "one size fits all" atmosphere so that everyone—man, woman, child, overweight, underweight—becomes an important part of the organization of the dojo. Acceptance in such an organization gives members personal satisfaction by compensating for any deficits outside the dojo.

When it is time for class to begin, the senior man signals the beginning of formal training. Students who have arrived early and eagerly await the beginning of class quickly form ranks. The highest-ranking students move to the left of the instructor. Others are situated according to rank in straight lines close together in a militaristic posture. Suddenly, without a sound, everyone drops to the floor in a formal position ready to bow because the instructor has entered the dojo. When the instructor is ready, the senior student calls the command to bow to the teacher. The teacher returns the bow, and class begins.

Frequently, a high-ranked or respected sensei will take several minutes after the students are in the kneeling position (a very uncomfortable position with the feet situated underneath the body) before entering the class and returning the bow, thus testing students' patience and endurance. Some venerable instructors institute a chain of communication, from high belt to low belt, in addressing the class. Only the highest-ranked and most-dedicated student may speak directly to the sensei.

After a period of exercise, instruction in karate technique begins. The teacher, calling out the proper phrases, instructs the class in both manner and method of technique. Students are expected to imitate each motion of the instructor. Each student works long and hard to perfect his technique and gain recognition from the teacher. Certain outstanding pupils, or "pets," receive much attention from the sensei and usually are made aware of their abilities.

Basic instruction consists of a series of universal techniques, including blocking and attacking methods, that are practiced in most dojos. The techniques are arranged so that they physically exhaust the student as well as develop the student's skill.

After students demonstrate proficiency in the basics, they are taught *kata*, prearranged fighting dances. Beginners usually are awkward in attempting to perform the kata. Advanced students who have moved beyond mere mastery of the movements seek personal enlightenment and mental transportation from the state of mind the performance produces.

While performing kata, students visualize imaginary opponents and simulate actual combat. The exercise encompasses a series of stylized routines executed in a traditional, prearranged pattern. Kata mimics true life-and-death combat and, in enacting the dance, the student is able to take the role of the ancient samurai. A skilled kata practitioner can produce a convincing illusion of being involved in physical combat with an opponent. Students who are adept at kata are accorded special deference, and they in turn tend to adopt an attitude of superiority over students who have not demonstrated the same degree of skill.

The third area of instruction is practice in *kumite*, or freestyle fighting. During freestyle, one student prepares to meet another in mock combat. The participants first bow to the referee, then to one another. The referee gives the command *"Hijame!"* to begin. The fighters attempt to gain points by striking at target areas (head or front of body above the waist and sometimes the groin) with a suitable offense (a ridge hand, straight punch, front kick). Because actual contact in these matches would cause injury, each opponent pretends to hit the other.

Although kumite is only play fighting, some students may embellish the dramaturgical (acting) aspects of the bout to their own advantage. Loss of control means disqualification, so a student may act as though he had been hit hard to cover up a lapse in control. Similarly, he may dance around to give the illusion that he is in better command of the bout than he actually is. Such theatrical antics are intended to disguise defects in techniques and win the approval of viewers. Whereas good performers gain recognition from other members, the performance of poor fighters receives criticism and their group acceptance may be significantly eroded.

The main instructional method is learning by rote: The instructor sets the example for students to follow. In learning a new technique or principle, students attempt to mimic the instructor's voice and ape the instructor's every move. Students are expected to perform the techniques over and over again until the sensei is satisfied with the performance of every student in the dojo. Many of the early dojos were staffed by Asian Americans who spoke very little English. As a result, students tended to memorize the movements without a clear explanation of purpose. What's interesting is that many first and second generation sensei continued to teach in a similar manner.

In keeping with the Japanese concept of education and their perspective of social responsibility, karate assigns a higher priority on imposing a strong sense of conformity on the student than on encouraging the expression of individuality. As the instructor defines the performance of each technique through acting out the part, students respond with a group effort in an attempt to perfect their own proficiency in individual skills. As students perform the techniques, advanced students or assistant instructors usually are available to show students exactly how the technique should be performed or reinforce a student's action by agreeing that his techniques are valid or appropriate.

During class, students begin to receive recognition of their acquired skills. Because the emphasis is on achieving higher ranks, students often form particular groups or cliques that serve several purposes. The members of a particular clique tend to congregate to avoid mixing with students in lower belt ranks. Having achieved status and prestige by virtue of their belt color and corresponding skill, students of higher belt ranks serve as examples for lower ranks. Realizing that lower ranks will emulate them, those with higher belt ranks may engage in light kumite or practicing techniques. Although they may look as though they are simply practicing technique, they often do so to impress others with their abilities. Members of a clique may exchange impressions of outstanding performers or discuss their persuasions and prejudices about such matters as the *bunkai* (translation) of the kata. Such an exchange tends to reinforce group attitudes and posture. Cliques also act as pressure groups to enforce expected modes of conduct.

Status groups composed of the highest-ranking members of the class make a point of acquainting new members or visitors with the dojo. As class representatives, they present a favorable image by virtue of their respective skills for persuading visitors to join the class. So also, they act as a greeting party for unwelcome visitors, sometimes called spies, who come to the dojo to steal techniques or challenge dojo members.

Dealings with spies usually result in an invitation to join in kumite competition in which the class champion attempts to defeat and humiliate the opponent. Or the entire class may choose to simply ignore the spy. The possibilities of encountering a spy from another dojo are great because it once was common practice to attempt to steal secret techniques from other dojos. These minor incidents serve to give in-group cohesion to those in the dojo. These and other similar incidents effectively socialize the person into particular roles that reflect the collective solidarity of the student group. The dojo (kumite) champion is supported in his role in that he serves an important group function in representing the skill, thus the honor, of the group.

Each person—whether the champion, the spy, or supporting dojo members—interacts in an elaborate behavioral configuration tempered by the cultural norms of the group. To this extent, the dojo's formal organization provides an alternate status universe for its members, which is limited to the confines of the dojo. In the dojo, students may achieve status and prestige otherwise unavailable to them in society. An important and added dimension is that, as the student achieves rank and prestige in the dojo, he may be able to translate this new self-concept into improved avenues for success in everyday life. Thus the child black belt becomes the class scholar, and the adult black belt, lacking formal college education, becomes the professional martial arts instructor or school owner and manager.

Some dojos have been known to require students to achieve superior academic grades before testing for advanced belts. This practice of fostering an improved self-concept is a by-product, if not a direct mission, of formal training in the classical karate dojo.

Although clique membership is a common method for achieving recognition, success in free sparring and general appearance constitute other alternatives. Even though advanced rank usually indicates fighting prowess, it is not uncommon for a white belt who is particularly strong or large to beat an advanced belt in competition. If the lower rank defeats a brown or green belt, he usually is ignored by higher ranks and congratulated by his own peer group, reinforcing the concept that, in the traditional dojo, belt color or rank represents avenues of achieving prestige regardless of external indicators such as winning a fight.

In addition to the student's appearance, the performer's manner (expressions that suggest a performer's demeanor or mood) further indicates each person's position in the dojo. The traditional karate gi, depending on its condition, is an indicator of prestige. The gis worn by beginners in the early dojos usually were large and almost yellow in color. As the gi is repeatedly washed it becomes whiter and more limp, and it tends to cling to the body as if to give a tailored effect. Similarly, the belt, as it is dyed to change colors as one advances in rank, becomes very loose and somewhat frayed.

The karateka's hands are true indicators of his years of dedication. A common practice for toughening and strengthening the hands is to strike the *makiwara* board. Over time, calluses form on the knuckles, giving the hands a weaponlike appearance. Although students remove the gi after practice, the hands continue to give the student recognition. Callused knuckles are a certain indicator of dedication and potential superiority should the karateka encounter aggressive people.

The equating of the karateka's hands with lethal weapons may be attributed to the popular but perhaps misleading practice of breaking inanimate objects such as boards, bricks, stones, and ice. Post–World War II karate instructors, both Asian and American, used the art of *tamashiwara* to attract attention to their demonstrations of the art of karate. Tamashiwara, a testing of the spirit, presents the art of breaking with bare feet and hands. Although these 1950s to 1960s karate experts intended to demonstrate the spiritual practice that has been popularly termed "mind over matter," the audience inadvertently misconstrued the performance to be solely a demonstration of the intended lethal effect of karate applied against an attacker; thus, the karateka's hands were considered by many to be likened to lethal weapons.

During the class routine, the student becomes acquainted with the formal organization and culture of the dojo. During practice sessions, the student registers new moves, learns new ideas, and displays his knowledge of technique and etiquette in an attempt to gain acceptance from his peer group. As each three-month practice period ends, students prepare to be examined. The student's progress through the ranks totally depends on his success during the promotion.

PROMOTION

Whereas the class routine may be viewed as a series of dress rehearsals in which students perfect technique and learn their parts, the karate promotion is the final stage performance in which heroes are born and future roles are established. The standard method of conferring rank is the examination. During the examination, students, instructors, and referees take utmost care to ensure that everyone knows his part. Visitors often come to watch this examination. Although such visitors have no vote in final decisions, their acceptance is desirable.

Students usually arrive before the exam and practice their techniques. At times students who know ahead of time that they will be tested together may rehearse a free-sparring sequence. Because free sparring is spontaneous and unrehearsed, the referees usually recognize who is actually sparring and who is awaiting a cue to attack, which would suggest pretesting rehearsal. The students' gis are especially clean and neat, and many students starch their gis for extra snap. In general, candidates for promotion are quite active as they try to rid themselves of stomach butterflies. Each student is expected to do his best because it will be three months before there is another chance to test.

When the sensei enters the dojo, the students hurriedly line up and are particularly careful to find the correct order in the lines. Exam time is a special time for the sensei, who usually wears a kimono over his karate gi. Honored guests and fellow examiners arrange themselves in a line with the sensei, and the formal examination begins. After a brief introduction of guests, the sensei addresses the candidates, bows, and takes his seat at the head of the dojo. One by one, students perform for the sensei: first the white belts, then the intermediate students, then the advanced students. During the exam, waiting students remain seated and refrain from talking.

After students demonstrate basic techniques, perform katas, and break boards and tiles, the student receives his final chance to perform as the freestyle sparring exam begins. During freestyle, those who truly have learned the ways of the warrior attack with total commitment. Weaker or more timid students are easily defeated and usually fail the test. During the exam the period of kumite emphasizes survival of the fittest, ensuring that only a select few will advance in rank. The exam signifies a trial by ordeal, after which successful candidates partake in the rites of passage symbolically dealt with by the ritual of the exchange of belts during the awards ceremony. This process is not unlike the issuance of flight wings to the aviator or the ceremonial stripping off of the boots and then hurling them in the air practiced by naval recruits. When the exam is completed, students form lines and bow. The sensei then dismisses the class and retreats to his office to grade exams. Visitors and guests usually congratulate the students who have performed skillfully and reassure them that they did their best.

When the class meets again, the sensei reads the list of candidates who successfully passed the exam. Upon hearing his name announced, the student falls into line for the presentation of belts during the awards ceremony. The lower ranks are called first. For the white belts, the chance to wear a colored belt represents an adequate reward for hours spent in the dojo. The green and blue belts are happy to have received promotions, but their excitement is more restrained as they attempt to display a posture of maturity and refrain from displays of delight and congratulations.

Once the socialization process required for attainment of the black belt is completed, it is never forgotten.

Promotion has special meaning for the brown belts of first kyu who receive their first dan black belts. Whereas kyu refers to youthful advocate, dan rank reflects full maturity. The years of work and dedication in the dojo require much discipline, and the results are significant.

According to Japanese social tradition, it can be argued that discipline in all Japanese traditional arts is so demanding that it tends to reshape the student completely, mentally and physically. As one master of Japanese arts related, a man who has attained mastery of an art reveals it in every action.

This change in character is perhaps the most significant part of martial arts training. The process of reshaping the person to fit the image of the warrior—trained in proper etiquette, skilled in the martial arts, and loyal to his sensei or dojo—begins with the initial lesson and continues to develop. The entire karate culture is directed to this end. The dojo provides a setting that facilitates the socialization process and enhances the student's responsiveness by separating the student from his routine of social life. Once the student is admitted into the dojo, the organizational structure maintains his allegiance through peer group pressures. Dojo groups tend to develop and maintain norms that circumscribe certain philosophical postures and encourage values to sharpen the person's perceptual acumen. Membership in the dojo group gives the student ego reinforcement from significant others. Eventually the student comes to inculcate the values of the dojo and strives to bring about the total integration of these values as he achieves maturity in the sport.

Membership in dojo cliques and participation in other karate activities—promotion, class routine, initiation—entail the development of skills that only a few may actualize. To this extent, nonmembers are recognized by their inability, whereas members are recognized for their displayed abilities and status. The total process in which students are socialized may be compared to the process used by adolescent gangs and various youth organizations. Just as members of adolescent gangs may develop skills and values that affect their adult lives, karate students recognize their own distinctive skills and values.

Of course, the values held in high esteem in the traditional dojo reflect the values of society: be a good citizen, give your life for your country, dedicate your future to success. Because of the rigors of training and the sacrifices students make to develop skills and progress in rank, students tend to remember the effects of training and practice throughout their adult lives. Most students do profess a change in attitude and character development. Once students complete the socialization process, they never forget it.

Though the promotion to first-degree black belt signifies status in the dojo, it can in no way be considered the final stage. As the karateka removes the brown belt and accepts the black belt during the promotional ceremony (signifying a ritual death of the former student and the emergence of a new person), he anticipates a future life in the dojo. Black belts are expected to become teachers and propagate the art as they continue to progress through the organizational hierarchy. Wearing the black belt and displaying a mastery of student skills, the new *shodan* (first-degree black belt) now may prepare to assume the honored title of sensei. Again and again, he will engage in combat rituals, striving for perfection and symbolically growing weary with the battle, because he seeks only peace.

Here, then, is the traditional dojo—the foundation for all modern karate dojos. Because the ultra-traditional dojo could turn out only a few graduates, it is often considered unproductive by 21st-century standards. In today's professional dojos, a student enrollment of 250 or more is considered average. In most modern dojos, an emphasis on pageantry and ritual has given way to an emphasis on utility. Although the overall structure has been maintained, each structural component may be altered. For example, the chain of command may be less militaristic to allow for more freedom of expression and to provide a more positive and relaxed learning environment. Certain practices, such as knuckle conditioning, may have been deleted entirely. New, more efficient training aids and advances in educational procedures have resulted in a system that can produce equally efficient students in greater numbers.

In the next chapter we will see how the rigid structure of the traditional dojo led to a revolution in paradigms, which has directly affected the performance of karate worldwide.

Development of American Karate

Asian countries are credited with originating a sophisticated way to use your unencumbered hands and feet as devastating weapons of defense. In many modern American dojos, ancient traditions have been updated and repackaged. Although new methods might resemble the ancient tactics, they're significantly different in performance and goal. Americans using their contemporary karate skills often win bouts against Asians using more traditional skills.

The dojo, once pregnant with trappings of Eastern mystique and economically designed to advantageously use the hardwood floors and aged window spaces to accommodate winter winds as agents of discipline, has been replaced by production model athletic clubs complete with saunas, air conditioning, and health food stands. For the uninitiated, the plush comfort of the American schools may suggest an air of laxity and freedom; however, the rigors of skill development require discipline equal to that in the Orient, promote status and authority systems similar to Oriental rituals, and develop karate athletes considered by many to be the finest in the world.

The development of American karate led to the introduction of a new industry that caters to the needs of the modern-day sport enthusiast. Specialized equipment including combative gear and associated paraphernalia is employed by contemporary karate practitioners in their activities. The sport has also promoted its own popular heroes, including Bruce Lee, Chuck Norris, "Billy Jack," and "Kwai Chang Caine." Collectively, martial arts masters earn millions of dollars from the movie, television, and printing industries as fans anticipate the premiere of each new feature film, television series, karate bout, or magazine highlighting scenes of stars performing their skills.

DEFINING AMERICAN KARATE

For the purpose of our discussion here, we'll separate modern American karate from the ultratraditional Japanese dojo, described in chapter 1. There are similarities, but the landscape of modern martial arts schools has been significantly influenced by the demands of modern American society. The practice of American karate may be loosely defined as a systematic method of punching, kicking, and grappling in which various degrees of contact are required and during which practitioners attempt to win victories over their opponents. Modern karate represents a mixing of skills and practice methods; thus, it often is referred to as eclectic, nonclassical, freestyle, or independent American karate. Moreover, many of the more traditional styles have been "Americanized" or updated to include modern kickboxing, weapons, and grappling skills. In each case, an emphasis on realism, combat efficiency, and contact training defines the style.

Traditional styles represent neat, concise, and highly organized patterns for skill performance. In the traditional style, you have little room for self-expression. In contrast, the American style is independent of mandates that require exact duplication of traditional skills—you're free to experiment with new methods and create innovations. The American style is the art of self-expression tempered by the identification of the dojo.

Practicing American karate includes striking a sparring partner within pre-determined contact areas, attacking with suitable weapons (hands, feet). American karate emphasizes developing your body as a sophisticated weapons system. There's also a complex social system requiring conformity among participants performing routines. As you perform organized routines within the dojo, adhering to a precise process of progression from white belt to black belt, along the way you develop character traits that promote honesty, integrity, and discipline.

The practice of modern karate has been patterned on Asian systems but has evolved into a uniquely American interpretation. Unlike Japanese shotokan or Okinawan ishhin ryu, there's no single style of American karate (though most American schools do claim brotherhood or lineage with one or more Asian discipline). The mixing of styles and philosophies and the addition of methods and practices introduced by Americans might be better understood if we look at the development of martial arts in the United States over several eras:

- the traditional era (1956-1966), during which Oriental practices were closely observed;
- the progressive era (1967-1972), characterized by a mixing of styles and the development of competitive heroes;
- the contact era (1973-1980), brought about by technological advances, including innovations in equipment, in the martial arts practiced in America;
- the international era (1981-1992), identified by the open acceptance of multicultural martial arts;
- the reality era (1993-2000), during which no-holds-barred fighting gave rise to and emphasized striking and grappling skills; and
- the contemporary era (2001-present), partly triggered by the events of September 11, 2001, after which Americans renewed their interest in the original intent of karate: self-defense.

TRADITIONAL ERA (1956 TO 1966)

The Chinese probably were the first practitioners of Asian fighting arts in the United States, but a century passed before non-Chinese were instructed in the art of kung fu. The California Gold Rush of 1849 and the subsequent building of the transcontinental railroad created a tremendous demand for labor. American business interests filled this demand in part by bringing thousands of Chinese workers to the United States. After fulfilling their work contracts, many of the workers stayed, living together in enclaves that came to be known as "Chinatowns."

During the traditional era, emphasis was placed on recreating pageantry and ritual.

The first karate instructors appeared in the United States as early as 1946, when Robert Trias, an American serviceman who studied karate in the Orient, gave private instruction to friends in his Arizona community. It was not until 1956 that Ed Parker, a Hawaii native, opened the first commercially successful karate school in California. In later years, many Americans and Asians, who maintained strong affiliations with Asian countries, spread karate throughout the United States.

The development of karate in the United States during the traditional era provided a basis for future modifications as the result of problems in transferring an Oriental discipline to an occidental environment. From the mid-1950s through the mid-1960s, the art of karate was highly regimented, with much promotion of class or style identity. Just as in Japan, Okinawa, Korea, and China, the arts in the United States were practiced as close to traditional methods as possible.

Karate fighters who attended tournaments were often referred to as taekwondo fighters, goju ryu practitioners, or other characteristic terms linked to their styles. Individual identity was lost because styles were considered more important. Practitioners of different styles were easy to recognize because contrasting styles were recognized by gis with different insignia and karateka with varied fighting skills.

Japanese stylists of this era were known for strong front kicks and well-timed reverse punches. Korean practitioners, dressed in the typical Korean gi or "do buk" with black trim, were identified by their high spinning and jumping kicks. Generally during this traditional era of American karate, much emphasis was placed on pageantry and ritual, as the martial philosophy of this time viewed the style of the art to be superior to the person, who had sworn allegiance to his or her style and instructor. Moreover, during the traditional era, karate was closely associated to an Oriental stereotype popularized through earlier demonstrations by Asian karate masters.

The dojos of the era were staffed by former military instructors, Asians, and first-generation students. Some say that the highly regimented classes were maintained by military types who felt comfortable instilling a boot camp atmosphere.

Producing a Popular Image for Traditional Karate

Perhaps the first national exposure given the martial arts in the United States can be attributed to Mas Oyama, who in 1952 visited several Air Force bases demonstrating the ability of highly trained karate personnel. Oyama, who attempted to gain interest in the arts by demonstrating the power of his callused fists in breaking wood, bricks, and stones, inadvertently introduced the image of the Asian superhero. This image of karate as a mystical art form that allowed proponents to defeat multiple opponents and break inanimate objects was later exploited by karate instructors attempting to gain interest in their schools.

Apparently, American enthusiasts, raised on the fast-gun heroes of the movies, were willing to accept the challenge of developing lethal force through karate. As George Dillman, a highly regarded kata champion, said regarding the popularity of karate in the United States in the 1950s, "While they had

Breaking boards was often used as a method of demonstrating the power of traditional karate.

their samurai, we had Billy the Kid. Who's to say one is better? People identify with these things." Although the fast-gun hero of the early west had disappeared, the opportunity to relive the character through martial arts appealed to many Americans. Karate experts, wearing custom designed outfits and building a reputation based more on myth than reality, could have been identified as characters out of the pages of history books—"20th-century samurai," as one expert put it.

By the late 1950s, karate schools had opened throughout the United States. The art continued to demonstrate unprecedented growth through the next decade. The popularity of karate in the United States has been attributed to the need for self-defense instruction, the appeal of Oriental pomp and pageantry, the opportunity to engage in a physically and emotionally satisfying recreational pursuit, the popularity of karate and kung fu movies, and the exploitation of the art by promoters capitalizing on public interest by presenting the art in its most violent form.

Promoting the Image for Profit

A number of economically successful karate experts who introduced martial arts in the United States saw profit in its widespread appeal. In the 1960s, Americans were attracted to the foreign garb, the pageantry, and the violent performances of brick and board breaking. While some karate masters intended to promote only the benefits of karate instruction, the methods of attracting an audience associated the art with an Asian superhero capable of

Women began competing in karate competitions during the 1960s. Pictured here are champions Joy Tuberville and Phillis Evetts.

defeating multiple opponents. People reasoned that what worked for the superhero could work for them. Americans joined karate schools by the thousands, many motivated by the opportunity to gain a new identity: superhero.

According to tradition, the black belt was the highest level of achievement. Thus, some practitioners sought the identity of the black-belted superhero. As a black belt gained a following of dedicated disciples (a practice that could be likened to the traditional masters), he or she could challenge lesser groups for control of the steadily increasing numbers of practitioners. So much emphasis was placed on becoming a leader that the actual virtues of leadership were often misplaced. In the process of attracting groups to the study of martial arts, the once honorable arts had in some cases been distorted by those who projected a false and inflated image of superior fighting ability that simply could not be achieved.

PROGRESSIVE ERA (1967 TO 1972)

The second phase in the development of karate in the United States was the progressive era. American society has long been referred to as a melting pot in which people of many nationalities form a synthesis resulting in a new order. While karate practitioners had formerly taken much pride in promoting only the techniques or skills their styles had developed, tournament competitors of the mid–1960s and early 1970s began to incorporate skills from other styles into their own fighting styles. As a result, the fighters felt better equipped to fight a variety of competitors. Some of the top tournament fighters of this era were Chuck Norris, Mike Stone, Joe Lewis, Louis Delgado, Joe Hayes, and Thomas LaPuppet. These fighters and others were characterized by innovative ways in which they arranged and adapted their fighting skills to enhance their abilities.

One of the top fighters of the progressive era was Chuck Norris, who entered tournament competition to attract attention to his Southern California–based karate schools. A favorite of magazines and tournament fans, Norris eventually won the World Professional title in Madison Square Garden in New York. In the 1970s, Norris retired from competition and, with assistance from movie star Steve McQueen (a student of Norris), entered a lucrative career as a movie star, action hero, and television actor.

Norris enjoyed success in his early tournaments, largely because he cross-trained in Korean kicking skills and Japanese punching skills. In so doing, Norris initiated a movement to progressively mix the karate-style arts to develop a more competitive fighting style. Before Norris, most dojos in America closely guarded their systems and disregarded skills associated with other arts. After Norris demonstrated how to blend the arts to get a better product, the practice became commonplace.

While maintaining close association with traditional training methods, practitioners during the progressive era laid the foundation of integrating styles, which led to the development of what's commonly called American

Some of the top fighters of the progressive era. Left to right: Demitrius Havanis, Ed Daniels, Ronny Cox, Skipper Mullins.

karate. This development of a new system of karate practice, even in its infant stages, was strongly rejected by traditionalists.

As the practice of karate matured in the United States during the progressive era, some Americans found that by altering their personal fighting styles to accommodate new techniques they could improve performance against opponents bound by the belief that only set patterns were of value. However, practitioners who changed their techniques and abandoned tradition did not do so without cost. Once separated from the security of known styles, the practitioner was denied the right to advance in rank and often was judged unfairly by traditional stylists who wanted to see their own players win competitions to promote their styles and reprimand the disobedient nontraditionalists.

While these initial changes in training and performance were adopted by a select few, the practice of karate on the national scene remained virtually unchanged, because the practice of karate involves more than just physical skills. To change the course of martial arts history from what Bruce Lee called "the blind following of tradition" to a contemporary American practice encouraging discovery and performance of new skills, the belief in the validity and superiority of both traditional skills and those who controlled them had to be challenged and overcome.

Throughout the 1960s and into the early 1970s, karate practice in the United States prospered. By 1974, a marked decline in karate school enrollment was attributed in part to the economic recession, the death of kung fu superstar Bruce Lee, the cancellation of the *Kung Fu* television series, and general apathy on the part of Americans toward the practicality of traditional karate instruction as a viable means of self-defense. The problem was not that karate didn't work. The problem was that Americans had glorified karate experts as superheroes, an image based on fantasy and myth, not on reality.

During the traditional and progressive eras, practitioners wanted to look like karate experts. An ability to trick the public into believing that the simulated (and sometimes faked) karate techniques could work was facilitated by certain traditional routines, such as the kata and prearranged sparring. This

Fighters and masters of the traditional and progressive eras. Left to right standing: Ralph Castro, Ron Marchini, Alan Stein, Chuck Norris, Ed Parker, Skipper Mullins, Tonny Tulliners, and Greg Baines. Left to right kneeling: Arnold Urquidez and Mike Stone.

sort of "pretend practice" made the public, as well as many karate performers, believe in the infallibility of traditional karate techniques.

The kata, like most karate techniques, was considered a devastating display of power. At one time, the kata performer's power seemed so awesome that some thought he should not risk practicing with a partner. Rather, he should imagine defeating multiple opponents. This often resulted in the kata practitioner unsuccessfully performing during the spontaneous reality of actual combat.

When performed by masters with years of experience, kata techniques might work. However, what works for the master does not always work for the student. Although the practicality of kata for beginners as a self-defense tool is dubious, students believed that if the masters could use kata techniques for self-defense, so could they. When they discovered they couldn't, they became disenchanted with karate. They watched experts perform enviable feats they either could not duplicate or were not taught. When they were unsuccessful in duplicating the expert's feats—defeating multiple opponents, for example—they concluded that karate did not work, at least not for them.

In addition, methods used to recruit karate students inhibited enrollment. Traditional karate school owners were trained to scrutinize candidates by subjecting them to ill-advised marketing procedures. Traditional instructors at that time screened potential students via an initiation period during which

Skipper Mullins and Ron Marchini battle it out during a progressive era competition.

the applicant was required to bring letters of recommendation or referrals and demonstrate to the sensei a strong sincerity to learn the martial arts. Students often were asked to sweep dojo floors or run errands for the master. When the master felt that the student could be entrusted with the knowledge he had to offer, the student was then advised that membership had been approved. Students who paid money for instruction often failed to understand the importance of sweeping floors.

The traditional teaching method required the master to set an example through which the student would learn with minimal explanation. Using the method of teaching by example, the sensei would demonstrate, then expect students to mimic the action. Discussion was often omitted because the American sensei learned his art directly from an Asian master who spoke little, if any, English. In essence, nonteaching became the primary teaching method that facilitated the traditionalists' beliefs about learning. While the time-honored masters might have been successful with this technique, traditionalists perhaps less qualified than the true masters caused much confusion about traditional karate skills and the manner in which they should be practiced.

The attempt to introduce the martial arts without recognition of and modifications for cultural differences had been unsuccessful. Karate skills certainly had potential for the American public, but they would have to be significantly modified to be accepted by Americans. Since traditional karate allowed no avenues for change (in fact, traditionalists resented change), the potential acceptance for a new modern system of nonclassical karate became increasingly evident. During the contact era, the potential became reality.

CONTACT ERA (1973 TO 1980)

Despite minor changes during the progressive era, karate in the United States continued to maintain a traditional approach. Not until 1973 was the superiority of traditional karate training challenged on a national level. The followers of new training methods developed in the United States ultimately changed the course of American karate. The period from 1973 to 1980 might be called the contact era.

Three of the leaders of the contact era were Bruce Lee, Jhoon Rhee, and Mike Anderson. Lee, an international film star, influenced millions of people worldwide to study the martial arts. Since the mid-1960s, Lee had been promoting the rejection of traditional styles with an emphasis on whatever worked. Lee maintained that kata, a traditional training method that comprised nearly 40 percent of training time, was practically useless in self-defense. He likened the practice of kata to trying to learn to swim on dry land. Lee stressed the abandonment of traditional methods, which he called "the classical mess," and instituted more contemporary training that stressed conditioning and included boxing and judo techniques. Lee named his system jeet kune do, but at times he referred to it as nonclassical kung fu or nonclassical karate. Many of the advanced concepts that I have included in this book can be traced back, in part, to the nonclassical karate developed by Bruce Lee.

For Lee, the basic problem of classical karate centered on those who claimed to be great fighters just because they could break large objects and defeat several opponents in make-believe battles. Because a few practitioners such as Mas Oyama could kill bulls or break 20-pound stones with their bare hands, each traditional practitioner claimed to be competent in similar feats. Practitioners rehearsed fighting scenes to use when demonstrating their art, leading viewers to believe they could defeat multiple opponents in real-life situations. Lee found traditional training methods too regimented. Emphasis was placed on observing customs rather than on learning self-defense.

Pictured here are Jhoon Rhee, Mike Anderson, Jeff Smith, and Joe Lewis. Rhee, Anderson, and Lewis were important figures in the development of the contact era.

Actual self-defense was spontaneous and unrehearsed, which Lee felt to be the total opposite of traditional methods. Lee's warnings, initially ignored by many, eventually were accepted by thousands of American students who chose to develop more realistic training methods in which they could become more effective in the sport and in self-defense.

Lee's primary training method called for contact in practice sparring, which most practitioners were ill-equipped to handle. Although Lee had been promoting progressive ideas since the mid-1960s, it was not until 1973 that his methods were put to the test. In 1973, Jhoon Rhee, a Washington, D.C., martial arts instructor, developed and marketed the original Safe-T equipment, which permitted moderate contact without injury. Rhee was influenced by Mike Stone, who proposed the development of hand and foot protection for karate competitors. Thus, the stage was being set for a dramatic change in American karate that would eventually influence the development of karate worldwide.

The first tournament to require Safe-T equipment by all black-belt competitors, the Top Ten Nationals, was presented by Mike Anderson in 1973. In

Jhoon Rhee, champion Jeff Smith, and traditional era champion Mike Stone pose for a sports presentation aired by the ABC television network.

addition to presenting tournaments, Anderson published an innovative magazine called *Professional Karate* in which contact fighters were highlighted in order to promote acceptance of the new methods. In making contact, competitors found that techniques developed through traditional training, formerly thought to be deadly, were less effective than they had been led to believe. Again in 1974, Anderson featured the use of Safe-T equipment, this time in world competition in which participants were permitted to make full contact to targets above the belt using standard karate techniques. Americans who had adapted their training to effectively compete in full-contact competitions won in the heavyweight (Joe Lewis), light heavyweight (Jeff Smith), and middleweight (Bill Wallace) divisions, fighting against opponents from Europe, North America, and Asia.

Joe Lewis, the original heavyweight champion and a former student of Lee's, played an instrumental role in laying the groundwork for the world championship. One of the original proponents of American karate, Lewis introduced the art of American kickboxing in 1970 (in which he was undefeated in ten consecutive U.S. title defenses) and promoted the inclusion of boxing and other contemporary training methods in karate practice.

With the demonstrated superiority of American competitors in worldwide competition, much emphasis was placed on initiating new training methods that would ensure victory in future efforts. Traditional training proved less effective in contemporary competition, in which professionals fight up to 12 rounds of full-contact sparring. As a result, new training methods that employed functional techniques from various systems evolved into what has been called the American style of karate.

Social scientists have long recognized the importance of ideological and technological advances as functional components of social change. Lee and Anderson provided the ideological changes that allowed the effectiveness of traditional methods in combat to be questioned. Rhee provided technological advances—Safe-T equipment—that supported the testing of new training methods.

An Eclectic Style Emerges

While loss of credibility and diminished student enrollment took their toll among traditionalists, the introduction of a new sport, contact karate, attracted interest. This new method of karate practice, developed in the United States during the early 1970s, allowed participants trained in the symbolically lethal techniques of traditional karate to make contact during karate bouts. Encased in specially designed contact gear, participants often abandoned traditional skills to hit their opponents with cushioned fists and feet as often as possible. The traditional practice of bringing one hand back in a set position as the other hand punched, while suitable for noncontact bouts, was grossly ineffective. Likewise, the traditional kiai, or loud yell, was found unsuitable for contact karate competition, as a blow to an open mouth could result in a broken jaw.

When traditionally trained practitioners were matched in full-contact competition, most chose to abandon traditional techniques in an effort to defeat their opponents. While we might assume that early contact fighters realistically attempted to knock out opponents by using classical techniques, some audiences witnessed what has been termed a "martial farce," because traditional school participants could not effectively control their opponents, which resulted in unappealing brawls. Consequently, karate as a self-defense art was severely criticized.

The absence of popular cultural heroes such as Bruce Lee and David Carradine (who played Caine, a kung fu monk, in the television series *Kung Fu*), ill-advised marketing procedures, and criticism about the effectiveness of traditional training methods resulted in sharp declines in karate enrollment.

Until this time, practitioners of regimental Oriental arts maintained control of the arts through time-honored traditions focusing on Asian supremacy in self-defense. Karate and other Asian arts had long been promoted as devastating forms of unarmed combat. But during the 1973-1974 displays of traditional karate techniques in contact competition, the supremacy faltered.

The 1974 Professional Karate Association World Champions included Jeff Smith (light heavyweight), Bill "Superfoot" Wallace (middleweight), and Joe Lewis (heavyweight).

Traditionalists, secure in their beliefs that what they had worked, were fast to criticize nontraditional (American) practitioners in their attempts to develop new fighting styles. Many American practitioners deleted the more esoteric practices of the dojo and focused on realistic forms of combat proven in the streets and tournament rings.

By attacking the function of traditional techniques, American stylists could also legitimately question the Asian dominance that had long promoted the ability of traditionally trained karateka. In this regard, some contemporary practitioners noted that if Americans could produce a better athlete through new training methods, they also could claim the authority to promote a new style. For nontraditionalists, the years of struggling for recognition of a new style resulted in a major confrontation with traditionalists. In the end, contemporary practitioners were accorded their just recognition, and traditionalists learned from their own mistakes.

Traditionalists Versus American Stylists

By the mid-1970s, as traditionalists recognized that Americans (including Asian Americans) could produce a proficient karate-trained athlete, the manner in which they could compete with the contemporary American styles became a primary concern. At first, many traditionalists sought to ignore the contemporary movement. Others, in an attempt to regain the public's interest, called for a return to the traditional ways of offering instruction—behind closed doors, preserving the mystique promoted by such Asian superheroes as the characters played by Lee and Carradine.

The Asian superheroes attracted clientele to the karate schools. However, potential students often were led to believe that they could duplicate the heroes' skills if they joined the karate schools. Traditional instructors, who built their reputations on their identification with the Asian superheroes, were unable to satisfy clientele who expected to see their instructors duplicate the superhero-type moves. Moreover, most students could not achieve the popular image of the traditionalists. As a result, many traditional instructors closed their schools or went into private instruction. Most of the traditional instructors who remained successful were those who accepted the American belief in the freedom to express interest in other styles and sport-oriented competition. The ideals of traditional karate remained functional, but the popular image of the Asian superhero and the contempt for change had to be replaced.

Promoting the Image of American Karate

American stylists and contemporary practitioners who had won the right to promote their skills could now seek total freedom from Asian dominance in the martial arts. The leaders of the American styles sought to regain public interest through media exposure and an alteration of techniques to better suit American patrons. While the board breaking and more esoteric practices of the art were less acceptable, the sparring or sport aspects of karate provided a viable means for promotion.

In order to attract a following, appearances by highly skilled participants who had altered traditional techniques or developed new methods were scheduled during the late 1970s in the form of nationally televised full-contact karate matches. The new karate, emphasizing the sport, has received national attention since 1974, when the first World Title Bouts were presented by ABC in a special sports program. Contact karate matches continued to receive television coverage during the years as fans developed interest in both the new karate champions and the methods of practice.

As bouts were promoted, American full-contact karate continued to become more sophisticated. The idea that full-contact karate punches and kicks, as taught by traditionalists, would kill or maim was proved false. By the late 1970s, full-contact karate safety equipment was replaced by boxing gloves, and the rules changed to emphasize kicking skills.

The most celebrated fighters of the era included Bill "Superfoot" Wallace and Benny "The Jet" Urquidez. Wallace retired in 1980 as the undefeated champion of his division. Urquidez gained international attention by defeating Thai boxers and Japanese kickboxers. He retired with more than 40 championship defenses. Jeff Smith, the original light heavyweight champion, went on to successfully defend his title several times before losing a controversial split decision in his final bout. Joe Lewis lost his heavyweight title within the first year after scoring two back-to-back losses. A fighter to the end, Lewis attempted to make a valiant comeback several years later but was unsuccessful in the national title fight.

The effectiveness of contact karate proved that change and flexibility could be of value to the martial arts. Moreover, the superiority of American athletes served to introduce American role models as leaders in the karate field.

As the media exposed the public to American karate champions, the popularity of karate schools staffed by non-Asian instructors continued to grow. While traditional karate gained in popularity through tricks such as lying on a bed of nails and walking on sword blades, contemporary karate practitioners sought publicity via karate tournaments, thus promoting a sports hero—an image widely accepted by North Americans. The emphasis on competition in contemporary karate was reflected in both the actual practice of the karate techniques and the fact that the new style of practice, with new skills and new heroes promoting the skills, provided a competitive service offered by American practitioners who competed with traditional schools for a limited clientele. Proponents of contemporary sport karate and those who supported the traditional art each felt their instructional methods were right.

The concept of competition has long been recognized as a vital force in American society and has influenced the marketing of karate skills. The idea that competition breeds a better product is evidenced by the continued advancement of business enterprises that compete for comparable clientele. In an attempt to gain control of a limited market, some groups sought to ensure that their products or services became the standard by which others were measured. The dominant interpretation often exists not as a pure desire for knowledge but to facilitate the developing group's rise to dominance. Thus, the struggle between traditionalists and contemporary practitioners was based on more than the desire to provide realistic self-defense instruction.

After the introduction of karate as an Asian fighting art in the United States during the mid-1950s, traditional groups sought to maintain control of virtually all the activities of the practice. The belief in the superiority of Asian styles of karate—shotokan, taekwondo, wu shu, and so on—was maintained and promoted by Asian martial arts in the United States. A percentage of costs for belt rank promotion was often returned to Japan, China, or Korea, where the traditional masters lived. Since Asian countries maintained the traditional authority to issue rank certificates, promoting the belief that the Asians had the only legitimate rights to promote styles, American proponents for the most part continued to recognize Asian control.

The traditional styles of karate, maintained by Asian dominance, sought to preserve the arts in a manner similar to the practice of the arts in the countries of origin. The traditional arts marketed in the United States emphasized Oriental rituals, even though they had been proven to be less effective for realistic street self-defense. The classical techniques, as well as traditional instructional methods, were held to be above change; thus, those who attempted to change them met with aggressive opposition.

A new concept in practicing karate, which first gained interest in 1973, required contact in practice and provided an opportunity for division among ranks of karate practitioners in the United States. The credibility of American stylists was strengthened by the commonly accepted beliefs held by the American fighting champions, who had rejected classical karate and introduced contact fighting to standardized training routines. Additionally, the success of Americans such as Wallace, Urquidez, Smith, and Lewis in competition with karate fighters from Europe and Asia made the contemporary movement more visible. Moreover, the movie heroes, once portrayed as Asian superheroes, were now being replaced by American karate stars such as Chuck Norris.

Due to the problems in performing traditional karate techniques with contact (even though the practitioner is presumably learning to defend or attack in the street during which contact would be expected), the basis for practicing karate became the topic of much controversy. Traditionalists ignored contact problems and blamed ineffective displays on poorly trained athletes, thus defending their methods. Meanwhile, proponents of the new karate recognized a way to gain support for new training methods through the legitimate belief that nonclassical karate techniques are more realistic as an effective form of self-defense. Americans, for years ridiculed as disobedient nontraditionalists for altering styles, successfully seized the opportunity to promote a contemporary style based on experimentation and discovery, thus ensuring their position as world leaders in the martial arts.

INTERNATIONAL ERA (1981 TO 1992)

In 1980, actor Richard Chamberlain starred in the leading role of the television miniseries *Shogun*. The hugely successful series introduced viewers to Japanese history, traditions, and the martial art of *ninjutsu*, sparking a new era in the development of karate in the United States.

During the international era, Americans found interest in many martial arts representing different cultures. Stephen K. Hayes, perhaps America's most prolific ninja, introduced forms of the art through seminars conducted throughout the United States. Like karate, ninjutsu shared the Japanese traditions; therefore, it was readily adaptable to many Japanese karate styles. So popular was the art of ninjutsu that several magazines gave a majority of space to ninjutsu instruction. Additionally, television programs and full-length feature films, such as *Teenage Mutant Ninja Turtles*, were devoted to the karate-like art. During this era, many karate instructors sought to supplement their classes by offering ninjutsu instruction.

A second martial arts craze during the 1980s was established by a protégé of Bruce Lee named Dan Inosanto. Inosanto (a kenpo karate black belt who had taught Lee's art of jeet kune do), along with Remy Presas, was directly responsible for the popularity of the Filipino martial arts of kali and escrima. Inosanto devoted full time to traveling around the country providing seminars in jeet kune do, kali, Thai boxing, and silat.

The international era introduced new champions to the sport of karate, including Keith Vitali, Billy Blanks, and Steve "Nasty" Anderson. Anderson's career lasted 10 years, during which he accumulated more karate titles than any other competitor. In the late 1990s, Blanks introduced the hugely successful *Tae Bo* video series. Among the top women competitors were Linda

Denley and Arlene Limas in fighting, Kathy Long in full contact, and Cynthia Rothrock in forms. Rothrock went on to enjoy a lucrative career as an actress in martial arts movies.

Martial arts journals, always seeking increased readership, focused attention on many arts now available in the United States. The ninja craze, overwhelming as of 1980, faded within five years. Interest in martial arts instruction in the 1980s seemed to increase each time a martial arts movie was successful. Chuck Norris, the champion fighter of the 1960s, had become the box office champion of the 1980s with several hit karate flicks.

In 1984, the box office smash *The Karate Kid* portrayed a new gentle image for karate and attracted thousands of new karate kids and their parents to the dojos. It should be noted that both *Teenage Mutant Ninja Turtles* and *The Karate Kid* featured fight choreography by karate star Pat Johnson, who has had considerable influence on the way the general public views karate. Unlike the dojos of the 1970s, the new karate instructors were prepared to offer a variety of martial arts training and teaching techniques.

During the international era, karate instructors who once had been apprehensive about mixing two or more styles of karate were adding a variety of international arts from Japan, Korea, China, the Philippines, Burma, Indonesia, Europe, and Africa to their daily programs. The United States truly had become a melting pot for a plethora of martial arts, sports, and fighting systems. Still, the question remained: which skills were best for self-defense?

The answer to this question would be exploited by Brazilian jiujitsu expert and businessman Rorion Gracie.

REALITY ERA (1993 TO 2000)

The year 1993 marked the introduction of no-holds-barred (NHB) and mixed martial arts competitions in the United States. Rorion Gracie, head of the Gracie jiujitsu school in Torrance, California, helped organize the first Ultimate Fighting Championship in Denver, Colorado, in 1993. In this event and those that followed, fighters representing karate, taekwondo, ninjutsu, jeet kune do, boxing, wrestling, judo, jiujitsu, kung fu, muay Thai, savate, and various other systems were tested in NHB competitions.

After viewing literally hundreds of mixed martial arts competitions, the result seemed self-evident. Several thousands of years ago the Greeks found that in NHB competitions, grapplers had an advantage over strikers. If the grappler could successfully drop his head and shoot for an opponent's legs, the striker would find no satisfactory targets other than the top of the grappler's head. Strikers who attempted to hit the heads of grapplers suffered bruised or broken hands. Grapplers were successful in compromising the strikers' advantage (their punches), then capitalizing on their weakness (a lack of preparation for ground fighting). In modern NHB competitions, results were much the same. Grappling arts have much to offer modern karate practitioners.

As a result of reality fighting events, grappling arts became popular for several years. Most karate systems have now added at least some weapons training (stemming from Japanese or Filipino influences) and grappling skills (based on Brazilian and Japanese jiujitsu).

Other unique advances in karate instruction during the 1990s included the emergence of martial arts business associations that assisted instructors with learning or creating new, more efficient ways to develop their practice. Organizations such as The Educational Funding Company, United Professionals, the Martial Arts Industry Association, and the National Association of Professional Martial Artists have dedicated time and energy toward educating thousands of instructors about leading marketing, educational, and management techniques. The result is that new karate students receive better services now than ever before.

To keep up with current training methods, seminars and summer camps became big business during the 1990s. Leading the group was the Karate College presented at Radford University in Virginia. Predating the reality era (the camp was created in 1988), the Karate College became the premier mixed martial arts training camp, introducing thousands of instructors and students to a variety of arts, including Brazilian jiujitsu, sambo, kali, ninjutsu, wu shu, savate, hapkido, and multiple interpretations of karate and taekwondo.

Mixed martial arts competitions became standard programming for cable television stations. By the late 1990s, mixed martial arts events were attracting professional athletes trained in grappling and striking arts with no limitations in style. Some might claim that the mixed martial arts events reduced interest in karate instruction since no karate fighters had ever won the events.

Ultimately, the introduction of mixed martial arts training during the reality era facilitated a positive advance to interpretation of classic karate skills. Modern karate instructors are more knowledgeable of the expectations of the combat arena. Still, the major focus of true karate must be directed toward understanding the way. To paraphrase the late Gichin Funakoshi, the founder of modern Japanese karate, the ultimate goal of karate is not the victory or defeat—it's the perfection of character.

The first instructors for the world famous Karate College at Radford, VA. Left to right: Bill Wallace, Jerry Beasley, Joe Lewis, and Jeff Smith.

CONTEMPORARY ERA (2001 TO PRESENT)

While competitions and new training methods for mixed martial arts sports dominated the last few years of the 20th century, an act of international terrorism served to refocus American karate on the original intent of the art: self-defense. On September 11, 2001, Muslim terrorists from the Middle East hijacked several jet airliners and flew them into selected targets, including the twin towers of New York City's World Trade Center, which were destroyed, and the Pentagon in Washington, D.C., which was severely damaged. Thousands of people were killed in the attacks.

Many reporters and writers have referred to September 11, 2001, as the day America changed. Surely, leaders in the karate industry recognize the importance of their practice in helping people learn to protect themselves. Karate instruction has much to offer. Learning from past mistakes and adapting to future needs will increase the success of the art of karate in the 21st century.

The period following the attacks was filled with patriotism and reflection. It was a time in which karate instructors put aside differences and sought to improve the arts by learning from the past. Perhaps even more important than self-defense skills, karate instruction offers the devotee an opportunity to find inner peace, protection, and a sense of belonging within a socially acceptable organization. Our own history of karate in America has shown us that karate, when properly understood, is much more than training for self-defense. Learning karate is a step toward perfection of character, a release of negative emotion, and a desire to become at peace with one's environment. The karate dojo offers safety, security, and a sense of belonging in a time when, for many, fear is running rampant.

Developing a Philosophy for Modern Karate

The primary skills of 20th century karate developed as a result of blending classical styles. There is no single correct method of performing a side kick, round kick, reverse punch, back fist, or any of a dozen or more commonly performed basic skills. The individual performance of techniques varies according to the individual and the environment. Any attempt to describe the skills of modern karate begins with an understanding of the *essence* of the skill—that which makes a side kick a side kick—not on the exacting mechanical components of the movement.

Traditional martial arts have the core task of rebuilding the student, both to promote and to reflect certain values or ways of thinking. When students enter the classic dojo (see chapter 1), their whole being begins a transformation into the karate way. This process is completed over a few years, after which the student thinks, reacts, and moves like a karateka—and this is how it should be.

Peter Urban's classic book *The Karate Dojo* and C.W. Nicol's passionate autobiography *Moving Zen* tell of the metamorphosis resulting from life in the traditional dojo. The goal of dojo training is to understand, visualize, and appreciate combat in view of the cultural and philosophical premise on which the style depends. In other words, to train in a Korean style of karate means to think and act like a Korean martial artist.

The goal of every style is to transform the weak, the poor of spirit, the strong, and the violent into an image created by the style's founder. Everyone in the traditional style of goju ryu, for example, should think alike. The goal of every student of kyokushinkai karate is to take on the attributes of its founder, Mas Oyama. To gain rank in kyokushinkai, the student must exhibit the skills possessed by its founder. Breaking, fighting, and perfecting the basics are necessary for earning promotions because Oyama, a great martial artist, felt these skills were important for success.

To become successful, indeed enlightened, in a specific style, the student must develop expertise in the skills considered relevant by the style's founder. For example, Mas Oyama was a proven fighter. He intended to drop his opponent with one strike. So his original training methods centered on developing striking power, muscle mass, and the timing and confidence to make a single shot count.

Realistic contact allows one to discover which techniques really work

This is fine, but what if you're not really interested in learning to crush stones, kill bulls, or drop your attacker with a single lethal blow? What if you entered a dojo wanting to learn to perform high-flying jump spin kicks like a Korean karate master? If so, then Mas Oyama isn't the person you want to imitate in your personal training.

Every classic or traditional style is about setting and observing boundaries. Most traditional instructors ask their students not to go to other schools or tournaments. In fact, traditional karate values dictate that the master generally should reflect disappointment, even anger, with students who try another style or speak against the limits set by the sensei, sabunim, or sifu.

As we discussed in chapter 2, in the 1950s and 1960s traditionalism was very much the order of the day in karate dojos worldwide. In the United States, styles were separated. Korean and Japanese stylists were constantly at odds, and Chinese styles were for the most part unknown until the television series *Kung Fu* premiered in 1972.

During the 1960s and into the 1970s, karate practitioners had no safety gear. They did not practice full contact in competitions (except through fouls). Understanding the kata, or hyung, was the primary accepted way of understanding the style. A chain of command based on belt color was the order of the day, and breaking boards often was used to demonstrate the potential for lethal skills. A skinny, middle-aged man with large callused knuckles and a master's belt was generally accepted to be far more deadly than a youthful, Mr. America-sized athlete with large biceps and a kyu rank. By today's standards, things were very primitive regarding the validity of traditional karate for self-defense.

Fighting legend Chuck Norris demonstrates (*a*) the round kick and (*b*) the spinning back fist combinations that proved superior to traditional methods when used in competition.

Since the 1950s, at least part of the attraction of karate instruction has been the false belief that karate training could turn the average nonathlete into a veritable fighting machine. At the root of all karate styles (Japanese, Korean, Chinese, Filipino, American) is the premise that the skill can be used for self-defense. However, many schools place a low priority on acquiring expertise in realistic self-defense.

Some schools emphasize culture; students learn an Asian language and observe Asian customs. Another school might focus on sport competition in which students learn how to score points against adversaries. Some more modern schools recruit students who desire physical fitness and care little about trophies, customs, or self-defense.

Thousands of karate dropouts have left karate because they had one image in mind but entered a dojo that maintained an alternate view. Similarly, hundreds of karate instructors sought expertise in the application of karate skills for self-defense and unwittingly became indoctrinated in methods that featured karate only as a sport or a cultural experience.

In the mid-1970s, I conducted an extensive survey that, in part, sought responses to the question of why people practice karate. Respondents were given the choices of sport, culture, philosophy, fitness, and self-defense. More than 75 percent selected self-defense as their primary reason for taking instruction in karate. Today I would expect the response to be virtually the same. Karate means self-defense to a majority of people, yet they practice methods and techniques developed by people who lack an understanding of what is needed for success in the modern-day combat arena.

Just as schools differ in what they offer, instructors vary in their reasons for teaching karate. For the entrepreneur sensei, karate might be a business, a way to make a living. To the sports champion, karate might be an outlet for ego gratification, a way to win acceptance and recognition. For others, karate might represent an interesting hobby or a social group in which positive social interaction is of primary importance. When used for sport, the application of karate skills might be very different from similar skills performed by hobbyists or fitness buffs.

In presenting the skills in this book, I have attempted to design a method that applies equally to readers interested in the arts for fitness, sport, and self-defense. In so doing, I have sought to interpret the basic philosophy as originally presented by Gichin Funakoshi (1868-1957), the father of modern-day karate.

EMPTY HAND

Gichin Funakoshi opened the first free-standing karate school in Japan in the 1930s. Named the Shotokan, the Funakoshi dojo created methods and ideologies that have influenced the spread of karate worldwide. In particular, Funakoshi is credited with changing the ideogram for *kara* to mean "empty." Thus, karate changed from a battlefield *jutsu* art to a dojo art that emphasized the *do*, or way.

Modern karate employs the term empty (*kara*) to mean that the art is without manufactured or external weapons. The body becomes the weapon. More important, *kara* should be interpreted as "hollow," or without interior form. On a personal level, *kara* means to render oneself empty of ego. To lack concern for the self serves to better promote the group cause, ensuring the fraternal order of karateka.

Funakoshi provided two examples of the meaning of *kara*. First, *kara* is the equivalent of a mirror's polished surface. The mirror reflects whatever stands before it. Thus the master of karate is free to change or adapt to his or her environment or circumstances. Second, Funakoshi suggested that a quiet valley carries even very soft sounds. As the karateka becomes empty (his or her mind is free and unburdened by unnecessary thoughts), he or she can respond appropriately to any threat.

Readers of popular martial arts journals know that I have spent years interpreting the philosophy of Bruce Lee's art of jeet kune do (JKD). There are strong similarities in the zen-like references provided by Lee and Funakoshi. Lee studied the works of many martial arts masters, which may have included Funakoshi.

In his book *Karate-Do: My Way of Life*, Funakoshi discussed several principles that can be interpreted in a variety of ways. The traditionalist seeking to fit the world into a highly regimented order might see a different meaning than the nonclassical exponent of self-defense. As a sport sociologist, I might greatly appreciate tradition and how it affects social interaction and performance. However, as a martial artist I tend to identify with the nonclassical interpretation of self-defense arts. In my opinion, it's perfectly natural to reflect both the tradition of Funakoshi and the prudence of Lee within the same technique.

Above all else, Funakoshi maintained that the ultimate aim of karate was not simply victory or defeat. "The perfection of character," as Funakoshi called it, is the intended end result of karate. The traditionally trained karate advocate might prefer to walk away to avoid a fight—an often unconscious reflection of a superior character. The traditionalist need not be primarily concerned with the validity of technique but could still be successful according to the founder of modern-day karate. Moreover, actual combat might adversely influence the development of true karate-do.

I'm not saying that traditional karate-do skills are not valid for self-defense, but do understand that dojo conditions don't adequately reflect the chaos you might encounter in a street attack. Many advanced traditional skills have become so specialized that conditions must be precise in order to perform the skills. For example, it would be difficult for a karateka demonstrating focus and power to walk on stage and, without setup, begin to break boards and bricks. Also, it's unlikely that a karateka demonstrating mental control would choose to lie on one nail rather than a bed of nails as he or she permitted cinder blocks to be broken over his or her body. It wouldn't work. A successful demonstration of advanced karate often requires an environment and a window of opportunity that is difficult to find in spontaneous street conditions.

Lee viewed traditional martial arts as being not unlike a tomb that restricted self-expression. Lee felt that classical karateka become so immersed in following "the way" that they develop a dependent mind incapable of anything but imitation. Lee wrote that he felt his personal method (JKD) was a vehicle for personal liberation from the limitations imposed by classical karate.

To achieve status in a classical style, you must give up individual freedom and yield totally to the dictates of the style. In classical training, the greater the student's dedication and adherence to style, the greater potential for status in the art. A classical style requires students to approach combat as though they are the embodiment of the style. Classical karate often offers not so much the reality of combat but the discipline and perseverance to follow a path, even if it's the wrong one.

NEW TRADITION

Taking everything into consideration, it may be concluded that what has become accepted as tradition (submitting to the dictates of a style in the way we move, interact, think, and perform) is contrary to what Funakoshi put forth. To empty one's self has been interpreted as giving up one's self-expression by completely submitting to the sensei and his style. The students of tradition have not been taught to empty their cups but to fill them completely with the dogma of a style. While the practice might not necessarily interfere with the process of improving character, it does in fact significantly limit performance in self-defense.

In this book, I present a new tradition, based on the writings of Funakoshi and Lee, for the practice of modern karate.

Defeat the Ego

Remember that, according to Funakoshi, you should always have the opponent in mind. The enemy, the opponent, is the self. Without discipline, we quickly become complacent, lose desire, and become victims of self-indulgence. Karate trains you to accept opposing beliefs and avoid intolerance and prejudice. Unfortunately, karate instruction has a history of separation and suspicion of change. Some still believe they can't learn from other styles because the founder of their own style created the only one true way.

All styles were created by human beings, all with their own faults and deficiencies. All kata were designed to show how the founder of the kata would react in given circumstances. It's acceptable to follow one style, but always be aware that it's only one style—not the only style and in some instances not the best style for the situation. Self-perfection can be attained only when you realize that karate is a means to an end. Enlightenment is the absence of limitations brought on by style.

In full contact fighting, Americans discovered that, when used together, strategies from different arts could make a better system. Here, PKA heavyweight Ross Scott takes out his opponent.

Among traditional or classic styles, physical skills always have varied. The often-used term "traditional" is limited to social order: the pageantry and ritual associated with learning the skills, and accepted behavior patterns employed in the dojo. Unfortunately, the adaptation of physical skills often gets bogged down because people think that because the skills of a style have always been performed a certain way, it must be the only way.

This is why some traditionalists have become obsessed with performing techniques in one, and only one, way. We recognize differences in style by the way each style is performed through techniques or kata. It has become a tradition among founders of styles that they must seek to reinvent a technique to become recognized as performing a different style. It's the ego that seeks recognition, and it's the ego that we seek to lose in favor of emptying ourselves.

It's submission to the ego that results in a sensei failing to develop his own character and teaching students a method that simply does not work. In modern karate we should recognize that techniques have always varied both from school to school and in actual performance. The back fist that works well in the dojo might need to be altered to work in the street. Traditional karate can be a much sought-after practice ensuring character development, or it can become an excuse for not revitalizing a system, style, or training method.

Accept That There Is No Best Style

There's no one best way. You make a style work by selectively adapting each technique based on your personal attributes and the conditions under which the techniques are rendered. When you train, train with what Funakoshi called "heart and soul." You become unbound by restrictive theory.

Consider the concept of striking with the closed fist. In combat, sometimes it serves the fighter to twist the fist a certain way. Sometimes it serves the fighter to follow a particular line toward the target. Some founders of styles adopted a particular line or performance as the truth. Styles are based initially on the founder's opinion. The way the founder chooses is the "right" way to perform the technique. As students continue to practice a technique over time, the right way becomes the only accepted way. The technique moves from a good idea to a tradition not to be changed.

Each traditionally held style becomes a boundary or limitation. We can perform a technique only when we observe the limitations of the style. Karate becomes relegated to one style as the only correct style. This way of thinking is wrong. Modern karate should represent no particular style; karate becomes not a style but a necessary response to a situation with techniques that may at any given moment appear to be any given style.

Through my response to a situation, I may sometimes punch high and at other times low, sometimes with much speed and at other times slow. At times I will find it necessary to start my fist from my hip; at other times, it may serve my purpose to punch from my chin or chest. I should have no limitations in the way I respond.

Light heavyweight champion Jeff Smith combined Korean and American styles to develop a world-class fighting style.

As Funakoshi correctly reasoned, like a mirror I must reflect what stands before me. Similarly, Bruce Lee noted that we must respond like an echo. In describing his own system, Lee was fond of using the word "totality." For our use (which differs from the definition suggested by followers of Lee), totality refers to the total of all the techniques you have mastered. To "float in totality," another phrase coined by Lee and redefined for the purpose of this book, means that you make no preconditioned choice. You simply answer the attack in a way that is unrestricted by style.

In this manner, you can reflect the correct response as you become the echo. An echo offers precision because it doesn't have to make a conscious choice. When you make a choice, you recognize a limitation. If we limit our thinking to a traditional style of karate, we cannot empty our minds because we have chosen a particular way (the style) as our response.

Repose in the Nothing

While researching the sport of fencing, Bruce Lee uncovered the phrase, "repose in the nothing." Modern karate is a set of skills that can be interpreted in many ways. A boxer uses four primary blows, but the techniques are interpreted in various ways by different boxers. In modern karate we use the various strikes and kicks, blocks and patterns commonly found in all styles of karate. We must recognize that there are no limitations in the way we can perform. We'll never be reduced to using only the shotokan round kick or the goju ryu low block. We can use all interpretations and, as Lee would say, be bound by none.

Joe Lewis demonstrates some of the nonclassical karate footwork that helped to create a modern American style.

INDEPENDENT MARTIAL ARTIST

In modern karate, I seek independence from the limitations of traditional technique. In this new independent karate, I will have no particular way of performing any technique, except that when I perform the technique I want to make it work. Funakoshi asked his followers to avoid dogmatism, a belief in the authority of just one way. His students were instructed to adopt strong techniques from others.

Avoid the tenets of a style in favor of the totality of expression you may attain through independent thinking. My techniques will be an example of "formlessness." They will be subject to no particular form (style), thus incorporating both the American karate philosophy of using what works and Lee's phrase, "using no way as way."

My expression of karate will be the total of all the skills I have mastered according to the range of application, unbound by a single expression. In this manner, I will empty my mind of preconceived ideas about combat and simply answer the attack.

This new "independent" way of viewing karate might be difficult to understand for some who have grown up under traditionalism. It's really very simple. The side kick, for example, originates from the side stance or sideways position and uses the side or bottom of the foot. Shotokan karate stylists might expect to chamber the kicking foot by first touching the knee of the supporting leg when performing the side kick. Goju ryu karate stylists might prefer to chamber the side kick without the tucked position. An American freestyle karateka might choose no chamber, increasing the speed of delivery. Which way is the right way? Always choose the way that works best at that particular moment. Depending on the situation, each technique may be correct. Master the technique according to the dictates of your style, then be prepared to adapt the technique to all situations even if it means forsaking the limitations of the style.

Once you're free of the ethnocentrism derived from style prejudice, it's easy to see all the different ways of performing the side kick as possibilities, depending on the desired result. The best style of karate is the art that is not a style but an expression of all styles. Remember that a style is a set of parameters that create limitations. "My reverse punch must be placed exactly this way, or it does not represent my style," says the traditionalist. The independent stylist seeks to have no such limitations.

Currently the sport of karate features a practice known as freestyle kata. Competitors freely express themselves by kicking, punching, jumping, and stepping in any way that best exemplifies their personal attributes. There is no one best kata. The winner is the best performer. In actual combat, there's no one best style. The winner is the best performer.

As we examine the skills and practices of karate, remember that what you see is a performance that worked best for one particular situation. Your interpretation may be different and still be correct. If you understand my meaning, you may in fact already possess the empty mind.

Stance and Footwork

The often-used term *stance* can be defined as a position that affords the fighter the greatest opportunity to present a strong defense while delivering a successful offensive maneuver. Mobility is a most important characteristic. Hand position (whether the fighter prefers to place his hands high or low) and foot position (whether the fighter prefers to place his feet close together or far apart) will vary. When a target becomes available, the fighter must be able to respond immediately. When an attack is launched, the fighter must move with a sense of purpose.

STANCE

The stance used in karate often reflects the style. For the purpose of this book, we will examine only one fighting stance, also called an "on-guard" position.

There are four primary reasons for taking a stance: to gain position, to deny access to the fighter's targets, to prepare your defense, or to prepare your offense. In assuming a fighting stance, I may choose to step forward in an aggressive manner or to step back to appear nonaggressive, giving up space.

The modern fighting position emphasizes mobility. Note that the hands are raised and the reverse heel is off the floor. In this position, the fighter has all weapons readily accessible.

For sport and dojo practice, there's often little advantage to stepping forward or back. However, in self-defense I may choose to step back to avoid alarming the aggressor or to reposition to gain distance.

To perform the stance, turn 45 degrees away from the opponent. By turning away, you take the center line (imaginary line from the eyes, solar plexus, and abdomen to the groin) out of the direct path of your opponent. Lift your back heel off the floor to permit greater mobility. Place your back arm across your lower body for protection, and place your front arm in front of your body for better defense. By placing your front hand high, you're in better position to strike with your front hand.

If you're right-handed, you might prefer to position your strong side (your right side) forward to improve speed and set up your forward-side weapons (hand and foot) closer to the opponent's targets. Bruce Lee felt it was very important to fight from a strong-side forward position.

Most boxers are taught to put their strong or dominant side back. The advantage to this is that you can set up your opponent with a forward side and strike with your stronger fist when an opening appears. In self-defense, it makes sense to put your strong side back. This way you can use your front hand to grab your opponent or immobilize his or her defense long enough to complete a power strike.

From the ready position, the karateka can assume a front balance (*a-b*) or change to a back balance (*c-d*). The front balance is often preferred for kicks, while the back balance is preferred for hand strikes.

Karate legend Joe Lewis demonstrates the proper execution of the upper body defense in this modern stance. Note that the arm fully protects the upper body, and the elbows are kept in tight to protect the ribs.

The knife hand, back balance, is similar in function to the cat stance. Different styles of karate often dictate the preferred stance for predetermined circumstances.

The advantage of the strong side forward is that your stronger weapons are placed closer to your opponent, improving your accuracy and speed. The advantage of the strong-side back position is that you can improve accuracy by either holding your opponent or setting up your strike. Additionally, since the strong-side back technique covers more distance, it arrives with more power. Positioning either strong-side forward or back can be easily and quickly altered by simply stepping forward or backward to change positions.

FOOTWORK

Footwork, or mobility, is the key to making all karate techniques work. A popular karate saying, "He who controls the distance, controls the fight," suggests that mobility accomplished through proper distancing technique (footwork) is essential for combat. Certainly footwork is important.

Watching masters of footwork glide across a surface is indeed inspirational. With effortless momentum, they advance, angle left or right, constantly unbalancing their opponents and preventing them from getting set to hit. Masters of mobility use footwork as their primary defense. When the opponent delivers an attack, the master simply is not there. Before the opponent can recognize his or her mistake, the master of mobility closes the distance, strikes with authority, then repositions in an area that makes the opponent vulnerable and unable to attack. The master remains unapproachable, the opponent off-balanced and confused.

Traditional karate footwork employing wide, deep stances may seem contrary to modern full-contact or mixed martial arts fighting stances. No doubt, deep karate stances stem from the original need for karate training. If karate began as a form of empty-hand combat often employed as the only means to fight armed soldiers attired in bamboo body armor, then it makes sense that power was more important than mobility.

The karate fighter who could block an attack, then strike through bamboo or other protection with a callused fist, likely had a better chance against the attacker. On the other hand, the modern tournament fighter trained to employ lightning-fast, light-contact kicks would be at a disadvantage.

The saying goes that necessity is the mother of invention. Surely those who invented karate had a need for a particular type of footwork. A theme of traditional karate has been the one-blow, one-kill option. Perhaps it was determined that moving too quickly (dancing) reflected the traditional fighter's lack of commitment to the task of total focus for the one-shot victory. Early karate tournament fighters who were too quick to retreat and reposition (counterfighting) were often branded as "runners." Even into the

Note the differences in style demonstrated in this picture. The fighter on the left performs a wide, deep stance demonstrating force and power. The fighter on the right assumes a more upright position which offers mobility— a wise choice against a formidable opponent. In karate, a variety of stances often are employed.

1950s, American culture dictated that it was not sportsmanlike to move around too much. At a time when kicking was "sissy-like" and taboo, one was expected to "stand up and fight like a man."

Traditional Footwork

Traditional footwork is required for the proper execution of traditional karate techniques. To maximize power in a single karate blow, it's necessary to use wide, deep stances. In the 1970s, promoters came up with a method called "full-contact karate." Full-contact karate was not kickboxing, even though fighters eventually began to wear boxing gloves. Full-contact karate was an adolescent rendition of point karate taken to the limit. Most of the full-contact karate fighters were trained in traditional karate and schooled in point fighting. Their attempts to attain the one-strike knockout—an objective if not the expectation of classical karate—often were foiled by new, more mobile stances and footwork positions being developed as the sport progressed. The champions of the full-contact era were those who adapted to the contact and learned to hit and move.

To perform traditional footwork, maintain a low posture and slide your feet across the floor. Your legs should be tense while in motion and then fully flexed upon completion of a technique. Feet remain flat on the floor. Moving forward or back requires the crescent stepping formation. The feet are brought together and then apart, forming an imaginary "C" as you glide across the floor. Moving sideways is best accomplished by either sliding your feet on the floor or quickly lifting the moving foot up while advancing or retreating.

Modern Footwork

The objective of footwork is to quickly and efficiently move just enough to purposely strike, block, evade, and reposition to achieve success on both offense and defense. There are four directions to be considered: moving forward, moving back, circling right, and circling left. Any position desired must focus on balance and coordination of the hands and feet. You always want to position to strike and elude to make it difficult for your opponent to launch a successful attack. Position yourself where he or she is not strong; where he or she is weak, attack.

The classical fighting stance often requires that the back heel is flat on the ground. This position provides a strong grounded stance, but makes mobility more difficult. The best idea is to choose the right stance for the job and not be governed by the boundaries imposed by style.

In the mobile stance of modern fighting karate, the body is turned 45 degrees from the opponent. Hands are positioned to intercept an attack or to deliver a strike to the nearest target. The reverse heel is raised off of the floor to improve movement. There are four basic rules for stepping:

1. To move forward, move your front foot first.
2. To move back, move your back foot first.
3. To move left, move your left foot first.
4. To move right, move your right foot first.

Step and Slide

Sometimes referred to as the "shuffle," the step and slide is used to advance forward or back, slowly or quickly. The step and slide can be used to gain distance, invade space, or deceive an opponent into committing to an attack.

From a fighting position, move your front foot forward two to four inches. (In most cases, you'll move only two inches. However, using the same technique, you can lunge forward up to 12 to 16 inches, depending on your body size.) As your front foot advances, slide your back foot up the same distance. Maintain good posture and balance as you move. If you're outside of the immediate striking distance, lower your hands to facilitate movement. As soon as you enter your opponent's critical zone (within arm's reach), keep your hands up.

To move back, move your back foot two to four inches and follow by sliding your front foot back the same distance. Sometimes you can confuse an opponent by quickly shifting up two inches and back two inches.

The cat stance is often performed in classical kata. Defensively, the stance is weak since the head is fully exposed. However, emphasis is placed on quick, snapping kicks which are delivered easily from this stance.

Try advancing one step, retreating one step, then changing lead stances. When you're constantly moving, you stay on the balls of your feet. The heel of one foot is always off the floor.

Circle Right/Left

Since karate fighters use both right and left lead positions interchangeably, the rules observed for the right side also are followed for left-side movements. To circle right, move your right foot two to four inches to the right and slide your back foot two to four inches right. By moving your front foot first, you maintain the option of stepping back, keeping the same position, or continuing to move. To circle left, move your left foot two to four inches to the left and slide your right foot two to four inches to the left.

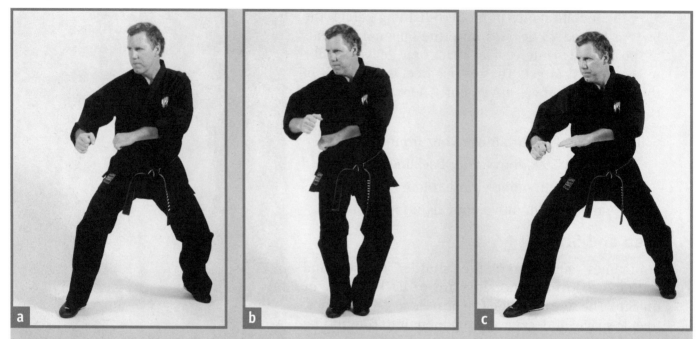

The step and slide is the most often used method for moving forward or backward.
To begin, slide the back foot forward (*a*), then step forward (*b*). To move back, use the same method,
but slide the forward foot back (*c*), and then step back.

You may choose to move fast or slow, with one or more steps. You may find it effective to advance two steps right, then advance two steps left, then advance one or more steps. The master of footwork is constantly moving forward, back, left, and right and switching leads to gain an advantage.

Switch Step

To change leads from right to left, employ the switch step. Move your rear foot back one step to initiate the change. Switch leads by sliding your front foot back, and at almost the same time slide your rear foot forward. Do not move your rear foot first except to move back. Unless you have ample distance between you and your opponent, refrain from switching leads as you advance forward.

In the clinch position, when both fighters have lost or nullified an offensive advantage, it is possible to use the switch step without the initial step back to push off an opponent and circle step or pivot clear of his or her offense. To do so, place your reverse hand on your opponent's elbow, switch step, and pivot on the front foot to turn your body out and away from your opponent.

Pivot Step

As you practice step-and-slide footwork, incorporate the pivot step. To practice the pivot step, begin in fighting position with either a left or right lead. Facing the wall in front of you in the left lead, pivot the toes of your front foot 90 degrees to your right so that you face the wall to your right. At the same time, rotate your right leg 90 degrees back until you have repositioned,

One way to quickly change directions when fighters are in a near clinch is to employ the switch step. The fighter initiates the switch step by immobilizing the opponent's forward arm (*a-b*). The fighter then pushes off the opponent to gain momentum for the switch of the lead leg to back position (*c-d*). This switch was used to set up a sweep and takedown.

facing the wall that was originally to your immediate right. Keeping your front foot in the same general area, practice the pivot until you have faced all four walls. You begin north, then pivot east, south, west, and return north.

After completing the four directions, pivot, change leads, and complete all movements in the opposite direction. In competition you'll seldom need to pivot 90 degrees. The pivot often is used to avoid an attack.

Angle Step

To practice angle stepping, assume a fighting position. Step forward in a 45-degree angle using your reverse foot. This procedure is used to reposition out of the immediate line of fire and is generally followed by a pivot step or an angle step in the opposite direction.

In this chapter, I have included the fundamental principles and tactics required for mastering karate. Practice with a partner in simulated attacks, with focus pads, and in sparring. Muhammad Ali coined the phrase, "Float like a butterfly, sting like a bee!" Avoid fixed stances, and learn to float across the floor.

Hand Strikes

The underlying premise of modern karate maintains that, when needed, the external parts of the body (most notably the hands and feet but also the elbows, knees, head, and other areas) may be used as weapons. When consistently employed as weapons, various body parts may take on a degree of specificity. Some weapons, such as the hands and elbows, are best suited for striking targets in the upper areas of the body, while other weapons (including those employing kicking techniques) are most sensibly directed toward targets of the lower body. However, at times any weapon may usefully be employed against any target on the human body.

What distinguishes one weapon from another—for example, a back fist from a hook punch—is the path traveled from point of origin to point of impact. Using this method of analysis, it's pretty simple to distinguish a round kick from a hook kick, for example, or a front kick from a back fist. Regardless of how a particular strike is performed, it need only travel the predetermined path to achieve recognition.

Again, remember that different karate schools, both classical and contemporary, might expect students to perform basic techniques in different manners. This does not mean that there isn't enough commonality among techniques for us to describe each kick or punch used in modern karate. To simplify matters, table 5.1 illustrates the paths of the most common hand strikes.

Charting the paths of common karate skills requires an understanding of two principles: the line of attack and the point of impact. The line of attack is an imaginary line from the attacker's body to the intended target. Usually, the line of attack is visualized as an imaginary line from the attacker's forward shoulder (assuming the fighter is in a side stance) or point of center to the opponent's shoulder or point of center. The point of impact is the target.

TABLE 5.1 Paths of the Most Often Employed Hand Strikes

Hand skills	Characteristics
Back fist	Strike with back of knuckle from inside line of attack (LOA) to point of impact (POI)
Fore-fist strike/Jab	On LOA, similar to stiff jab
Ridge hand	Outside LOA, utilizing the ridge of the hand, arm straight
Hook	Similar to ridge hand, but with closed fist on smaller arc, arm bent
Reverse punch/Cross	On LOA from reverse side
Low block	Protects lower body
Middle block	Used against classical mid-punching
High block	Defense against high attack
Knife hand/Chop	Chop with side of hand (open)

As we examine each punch or kick, we'll refer to the line of attack and the point of impact in relation to the specific technique.

The outcome of any technique is determined in part by the variables of speed, power, and deception. If a strike fails to score, the fighter may choose to change the speed or power of the technique or deliver the strike in a more deceptive way. Of course, the fighter has the option of changing techniques as well. Note that in a spontaneous encounter, such as in competition or street defense, the delivery of the technique will often vary. There is no single best way to perform common strikes.

THE HANDS AS WEAPONS

Americans have long recognized the usefulness of engaging their hands as weapons. As a natural weapon, hands have been employed to grab, strangle, punch, or slap an assailant. However, it was not until the introduction of karate in the early 1950s that hands earned the reputation of potential deadly weapons.

The Karate Chop and Open Hand

The popularity of the karate chop, or open-handed strike, may be attributed to the introduction of Asian martial arts and their exploitation by the film industry. James Bond and his fellow movie action heroes greatly enhanced the mystique associated with the karate-trained hand. However, the legitimate base for the credibility and potential of the open hand can be traced to a number of Oriental masters. As noted in chapter two, the most notable of the early Asian masters was Masutatsu Oyama.

Oyama's training methods included year-long vigils alone in the mountains practicing his art. During his training, Oyama would strike a rope-covered makiwara thousands of times a day. Over time, he developed callused hands that could break 20-pound stones and large quantities of tiles, bricks, and boards.

In his battle with a bull, Oyama was able to tire the animal by wrestling it to the ground. With one arm around the neck and the other held high in the air, Oyama could then smash off the horn with his powerful shuto, or karate chop. Although this feat later was protested by animal rights activists, it remains a tribute to the discipline of one man and the power that can be achieved through karate training.

Tournament competitors of the early 1960s would often combine a front kick with a jumping chop to the neck of an opponent for a point. As a self-defense weapon, the chop is perhaps most successfully aimed at the neck of an assailant. While the chop continues to be a mainstay in the classical styles, most American martial artists emphasize boxing-style hand movements, limiting the use of the chop in both tournament competitions and studio practice. However, the classic karate chop remains a functional tool for self-defense.

The karate chop. Karate superstar Chuck Norris performs the karate chop in a demonstration with 1960s World Champion Skipper Mullins.

The heel (the bottom of the hand) is the contact area for the karate chop. Unlike the bare knuckles, the heel of the hand is sufficiently padded to provide cushion during contact. The swinging or chopping motion used in performing the technique allows the practitioner to effectively employ body weight in adding power to the chop. Additionally, the chop can be completed inside, outside, or on the line of attack to the point of impact, allowing for considerable versatility.

It's not necessary to condition the chopping surface of the hand. However, striking a bag or makiwara (rope-covered pole) improves performance. One useful method is to stand in fighting position with your forward hand placed close to your chin. Practice stepping forward and striking at the same time. By stepping forward at the same time as your chop, you increase your power. Be sure to flex your shoulder and twist your hip at the same time as you step. This gains you maximum effect from the chop.

The chop is best applied to the front of the throat, temple, side or back of the neck, or nose. If an attacker is behind you, a chop to the groin might also be effective. A chop to the wrist can cause an attacker to drop a weapon.

The Fingertip Strike

A strike to the eyes using the fingertips is one of the most effective strikes in the martial arts. If the karateka is successful in striking the eyes, the opponent is completely immobilized.

Assume a fighting position with your strong side forward. You can position your forward hand near your chin for a whiplike fingertip strike, or you can thrust your fingers directly toward the eyes without a chambered movement. All four fingers are ridged. Make contact in a direct strike or in a rakelike movement, as if wiping your ridged fingertips across your attacker's eyes.

The finger tips also may be used in a relaxed position simply by flipping the fingers up and out toward the eyes. To improve accuracy, begin with the fingers as close as possible to the opponent's eyes. A fingertip strike attempted from some distance has little chance of making contact, as the opponent will block or redirect your attempt.

Perhaps the most effective method for using the fingertip strike requires immobilizing the opponent's forward hand. From the fighting position, strike with your front hand. Permit your opponent to block your strike. Using your rear hand, trap or grab your opponent's blocking arm. You have now cleared a path from your fingertips to your attacker's eyes. Strike!

The fingertips also can be used for nerve strikes to the neck or to gouge or apply pressure to other sensitive areas such as the armpits, ears, or groin.

The Palm Heel

The heel of the palm has been used to break more than 1,000 pounds of ice, boards, bricks, and cinder block slabs. Much power can be generated when the heel of the palm is used as a striking weapon. The palm heel is used in some karate sports competitions as well as in other sports, including sumo, wrestling, and football.

The palm heel can be used with the forward hand in a strong or stiff-armed method or with the reverse hand in a thrusting strike. Assume a fighting position with your strong side forward. To use the palm heel, position your palm with fingers pulled back and strike forward. Step and use a twisting force (torque) at both the hip and forward shoulder to gain power.

Add to the advantage of the palm heel strike by using your fingertips to gouge the eyes after the palm makes contact with the nose, the most common target of the palm heel. The palm heel may also be directed to the ears or, with less effect, to the back of the neck or to other parts of the head. You might also direct a palm heel to the solar plexus by striking upward.

Karateka who prefer not to use the fingertip thrust or the closed fist may find success with the palm heel, followed by clawing or gouging with the fingertips, especially to the eyes.

The Back Fist

Joe Lewis, the highly acclaimed point/full-contact karate champion of the 1960s and 1970s, often is credited with popularizing the use of the back fist. Lewis's personal interest in the back fist developed through his association with Bruce Lee. Lee, who studied boxing and fencing as well as the hand-dominated style of Chinese wing chun kung fu, was convinced that forward-side strikes using a method known as "independent motion" presented the most functional maneuvers for the use of the hands.

The notes Lee compiled contained many methods drawn directly from basic fencing theory. The concept of independent motion, often employed in fencing, can be directly applied to sport karate. Simply stated, *independent motion* refers to the process in which the weapon—in this case, the back fist—is made to move initially without full-body motion. After moving the weapon first, the body is brought into play to support the technique and increase power. By moving the weapon in the direction of the proposed

The back fist performed with full extension (*a*) and performed in competition (*b*).

target first and deleting the chambered or cocked position used in traditional karate, speed is increased. Moreover, the explosive quality and deceptiveness of the forward-side skill is more fully actualized through independent motion.

After working with Lee in 1968, Lewis further advanced the use of forward-side skills—most notably the back fist, forehand strike, and forward-side kick—in tournament competition. Prior to this period, most competitors depended largely on the reverse punch as the major hand technique. However, as a result of Lewis's success and the progressive ideology that dominated the late 1960s, the forward-side strike gained acceptance in the American karate community.

The back fist (or back knuckle, as it is sometimes called) typically is performed by releasing the chambered or cocked fist in an arcing manner toward a target. The fist is directed from inside the line of attack and returns inside the line of attack. The fist may be held low on the waist or as high as the shoulder. Many competitors deliver the back fist without chambering, thus increasing the deceptive quality and explosive potential of the independently thrown technique.

Generally, the back fist is functional for self-defense and point karate but less useful for full-contact competition. Along with the reverse punch and the round kick, the back fist is one of the most often-used point karate skills.

Spinning Bottom Fist

The spinning bottom fist is a product of 1970s point karate competitions. While some kata employ a spinning hand strike, the technique did not reach its full potential until it was introduced in competition. By spinning your body, you can become decidedly more deceptive and generate considerable power. Such spin hitting is illegal in boxing.

From a fighting position, turn your body 180 degrees (one half of a full circle). You can move forward or step back to complete the strike. It's important to turn your head first, regaining visual contact with the intended target as quickly as possible. Avoid lifting your moving foot completely from the floor. For efficiency, partially slide the foot across in a straight line. If you strike by advancing, your reverse foot will slide across the floor. If you retreat with the spin, then your front foot will glide across the floor. The nonsliding foot simply pivots 360 degrees.

In some cases, it's acceptable to remove your sliding foot completely from the floor to increase speed. If you connect, the strike will achieve maximum power. But if you miss, you may be well off balance and susceptible to a counterattack. As you spin, keep your striking hand close to your body until you have complete visual contact with the target. A snap back generally is used in point competitions, and a follow-through is preferred in full contact or self-defense. The contact area often is the bottom of the fist, but the strike may be equally effective using the back of the knuckles of a clenched fist or the heel of an open hand. Whether you strike with the fist, forearm, or elbow, the effect is dramatic. It hurts!

The spinning bottom fist may be used as a single strike or in a combination of a jab and spinning strike. The technique is a natural follow-up to a round kick.

The Fore-Fist Strike

In classical karate, the fore-fist strike (the side closest to the intended target) is delivered by stepping forward and striking with a turnover or full rotating punch. Typically, the fist is chambered at the hip; in more eclectic styles, it is sometimes chambered at the chin. It's interesting to note that the point of origin or chamber position is a subject that causes great discomfort to some nontraditionalists.

Often, traditionalists are accused of keeping their hands at their pockets as they attempt to punch from the hip. Traditionalists counter that greater power may be achieved when a punch is chambered at the hip. In an unplanned self-defense encounter in which a split second may make a huge difference, it might well be the best choice to punch directly from the hip rather than take the time to place the fist up to the chin before completing the strike.

To perform the fore-fist strike, fully extend your arm so that the fist, elbow, and shoulder are on one line. Your hip and shoulder thrust forward as the step is completed. If your timing is right, the fore-fist strike can be the perfect answer to an attack.

The fore-fist strike, or jab. To perform the jab, assume a fighting position (*a*). By stepping forward (*b*), power and distance are added to the strike. Different types of karate might require that one hand be held next to the chin. Sometimes the feet are placed flat or, in this case, the heel of the back foot is raised to assist in mobility.

The Jab

Both the jab and the fore-fist strike are delivered from the forward side, but this is where the similarity ends. While the fore-fist strike is a thrust, the jab is a snap. For maximum efficiency, the fore-fist strike requires that the fighter step forward and focus completely on the single attack. The jab may be performed with or without a step and is often delivered as a single forward blow (without a swift follow-up or movement).

The jab is most often delivered from the shoulder or chin but can be just as effective when thrown from the hip, "Ali" style. For the contact fighter, the jab is the basic technique for feeling out the opponent, establishing distance and control, and setting up additional kicks and strikes.

From the fighting position, relax your fist and quickly snap your hand toward the target—most often your opponent's face but sometimes the stomach, gloves, or arms—and back again. Effective jabs are based on speed, timing, and accuracy. With a successful jab, you can chisel away at your opponent's defense, opening gaps and preventing him or her from effectively getting set to hit. An opponent who cannot get ready to strike will not be able to strike with power or accuracy.

In self-defense, the jab is used to quickly answer an attack and set up a powerful follow-up. The forward hand jab is among the most effective strikes in the fight game.

The Ridge Hand

Because it's very deceptive, the ridge hand is effective for both self-defense and competition. Experts who use the ridge hand technique often employ a broken rhythm in applying the skill. As the technique is delivered, it begins slow and appears to change both direction and speed as contact is made to the target.

The ridge hand uses the top or ridge of the hand and is thrown in an arc similar to a roundhouse kick. Because the opponent sees the technique coming, he or she naturally reacts to the initial speed and direction of the weapon, often leaning back or placing an arm in the intended flight path. The unique quality of the ridge hand is actualized when the counter is intercepted and avoided, allowing for the ridge hand to score.

The ridge hand. The top of the hand is used in performing the ridge hand (*a*). To add power, the fighter often steps back (*b*), placing the weight on the back side so that a pulling action can be employed.

Because you wind up to perform the ridge hand, a considerable amount of power can be achieved. An alternate method for completing the ridge hand is to avoid the windup and deliver a reduced pay load in a curving jab-like fashion. This type of ridge hand may still be effective when a torque from the hip and shoulder are employed for power.

The Hook

The hook shares the arcing motion in common with the ridge hand as it travels from outside the line of attack to the point of impact. The hook is one of the most difficult techniques to master. The fist may be positioned either in vertical style, with palm facing in toward the body, or in turnover style, with palm facing down. The power from the hook is generated primarily from the shoulder and hip since the actual hooking fist often travels less than 12 inches from point of origin (usually the chin) to point of impact.

As the hook is performed, the hip and shoulder must begin the initial movement. The hooking fist is then directed toward the target in a whiplike manner. It's possible to hook at the same time as the hip and shoulder are turning, but the hook will lose some of its snap. Attempting to hook without the complex body rotation yields only a slaplike effect.

The hook punch. Similar to the ridge hand, a closed fist (*a*) is used and comes across center line to the point of impact (*b*), usually the head or body.

In most cases, the hook is thrown by stepping toward the opponent. The hook also may be effective when stepping away from the opponent. While some advanced practitioners are able to use the hook effectively as a single direct attack, it's most often used to follow up a right cross or reverse punch.

It's extremely important to note that the jab, cross, and hook strikes used in kickboxing yield a different rhythm from the corresponding forefist strike, reverse punch, and ridge hand applied by strict karate practitioners. The mechanics of karate require a sort of lockout, with maximum focus applied at the last second. The mechanics of kickboxing avoid the lockout, preferring a snaplike effect. As a result, kickboxing versions of the jab, cross, or hook are better suited for competition, while karate techniques are perhaps more efficient for the one-blow, one-kill theory of karate.

Practice the hook against a heavy bag. Be sure to snap the punch (retract the punch immediately after contact) and reposition your body after each punch. Try the jab-cross-hook combination. The hook also can be used effectively as a follow-up to a probing jab but requires a higher level of expertise. The hook, though difficult to master, is an extremely effective technique.

In this series the fighter delivers the right cross (*a*), left hook (*b*), and right upper cut (*c*) combination favored by many full-contact karate fighters.

The Cross

When used in orthodox boxing (meaning left side forward), the right cross travels from the chin, across the body, to the opponent's head or body. The right cross may be the most powerful hand skill in full-contact karate, perhaps surpassing the left hook. Unlike the hook, the cross is relatively easy to learn.

To perform the cross, assume a fighting stance. Step forward with your front foot and pivot your rear foot so that your heel is off the ground and your reverse foot points toward the target. As the cross is delivered, twist your hips forward into the punch. To maximize power, drop the trunk of your body as if you're sitting ("sit on it," as it is sometimes instructed). The drop or sit lowers your body only an inch or two. In so doing, power from your body drop is focused forward to yield a greater pay load to the punch. Like all contact karate techniques, the cross is quickly snapped back to its point of origin, the chin.

In most cases, the cross follows a jab. In a few combinations, the cross is an appropriate follow-up for a hook. The cross seldom is thrown as a single direct attack. Practice the cross by striking a heavy bag. Be sure to snap the punch and reposition after the strike. Do not stand in one place and strike the bag repeatedly. Practice moving after each punch—as if you're involved in a confrontation and don't want to get hit.

The Reverse Punch

The reverse punch is performed by executing a straight punch from the side opposite the side facing the opponent. The reverse punch is deceptive in that it's hidden from the immediate front side. The fist travels on the line of attack and returns on the line of attack. Contact is usually made with the fist in a vertical position with palm facing in toward the body or in a turnover position with palm facing down. In some cases, the fist may be turned palm up in an uppercut motion. After completing the reverse punch the karateka, unlike the kickboxer, typically tenses the body while completing a kiai (shout).

The karate-style reverse punch has long been the top point-scoring hand strike in modern competition. Former 1980s world karate champion Steve Anderson relied heavily on the reverse punch to defeat opponents. Anderson's "California blitz" style reverse punch required a head-down lunging method in which bridging the gap became all important. Others fighters, including 1960s champ Mike Stone, would often set up the reverse punch with a forward-side blocking motion. When a block was unnecessary, the forward hand was often used to grab the opponent's gi and pull him into the reverse punch.

For karate-trained athletes, the well-timed reverse punch represents the epitome of the one-punch, one-kill mentality. The reverse punch differs considerably from the cross, although to the untrained eye they might appear similar.

The reverse punch. From fighting position, the reverse hand is delivered to the target (*a*). By punching from the back side (*b*), the strike covers more distance, thus delivering more power.

To perform the reverse punch, assume a fighting position. If you're right side dominant, you'll prefer to keep your left side forward to set up the right reverse punch.

In classical karate styles, the reverse punch is chambered at or near the hip. Nontraditionalists often refer to chambering at the hip as "keeping your hands in your pockets," but there is more to the technique than can be readily surmised.

While completing a degree at the University of Northern Colorado in the early 1980s, Dr. Richard Arlin Stull, now a university professor, conducted research regarding the influence of speed and chamber position on the reverse punch. In measuring the effectiveness of the reverse punch, Stull concluded that the term "peak velocity" represents the instant in which the karateka's fist is traveling at peak speed. Preferably, peak velocity is attained at the point of impact, transferring the greatest amount of momentum to the target (momentum equals mass times velocity). A punch that originates from the hip and covers an arm's length distance can potentially generate greater momentum than a punch thrown from the chin in the typical boxing method.

Classical karate. Differing from modern American karate in both form and function, classical karate is often preferred by the artist in search of the perfect performance. In this sequence, traditional Japanese karate is demonstrated. (*a*) The classical stance. (*b*) A deep chamber is required to perform the back fist (*c*) and the reverse punch (*d*).

Modern stylists claim that the classical styles are too telegraphic in nature and allow the opponent to recognize the technique before it is completed, thus making actual execution more difficult. Note the exaggerated chamber required of the classical wrist, or chicken hand strike (*e-f*) and the knuckle strike (*g-h*).

At a 1986 summer camp in New York, three former world champions were tested to ascertain a momentum score on a newly developed impact pad called Impax. While two of the champions assumed boxing stances and completed a right-left cross, the third participant performed a karate-style reverse punch chambered near the hip. The karate-style reverse punch measured significantly higher impact.

While the karate reverse punch typically travels a longer distance, generating a slower average velocity and a maximum peak velocity, it can be a more powerful strike than the boxer's right cross. Sometimes it's acceptable to complete the long focused reverse punch (in breaking, for example). In self-defense or competition, a faster average velocity achieved by reducing the distance traveled may result in a more effective conclusion. In other words, when you have time, punch from the hip for maximum power. When you don't have time, perhaps due to an attack, opt for the faster response, punching from the chin.

As the reverse punch is completed, thrust your hips forward and drop your body weight for added power. Some traditionally trained karateka have begun to raise the reverse foot off the floor instead of placing the reverse foot flat. If you choose the traditional format for the reverse punch and have time to complete the focused technique, then by all means plant both feet squarely on the floor.

It may seem contrary to suggest that you should contemplate repositioning and snapping the reverse punch. Many karateka have experimented with various combinations of the modern cross and the traditional reverse punch. If a method consistently works for you under varying conditions, then consider adding it to your arsenal. Classical hand strikes, when conditioned by vigorous makiwara training and performed in wide, deep stances, can be devastating. A callused fist can break an attacker's bones, resulting in a one-punch victory. On the other hand, the nonclassical jab, cross, and hook combined with an upright mobile stance has equal effect in striking the attacker into submission. Both ways are effective. As you master karate, keep an open mind and use what works best for you.

Kicks

The art of kicking varies widely among karate styles. Practitioners of specific styles of karate often are limited to performing those kicking skills accepted as part of their styles. The Korean karate expert accustomed to high-flying spin kicks may cringe at the site of a Japanese-style spinning hook. Similarly, the economically minded wado ryu stylist might consider the tang soo do practitioner's high kicks unnecessary antics.

Some karateka choose to venture outside the boundaries of style to perfect their kicking potential. Former full-contact karate champion Bill "Superfoot" Wallace initially trained in a style of Okinawan karate known for low snap kicks. Wallace's natural flexibility permitted him to develop his own kicking method. Wallace's kicking ability far surpassed most other karateka, regardless of style. So popular was Fast Billy's left leg that it was assumed when he passed on to that great dojo in the sky, his left leg would be placed on permanent reserve in the National Martial Arts Museum.

Kicking finesse does play a major role in differentiating karate styles, but kicking ability also has greatly enhanced individual success. Perhaps the first super kicker was Texas legend Skipper Mullins. Tall, tough, and lanky, Mullins earned a world lightweight title in the 1960s through his incredibly fast kicking ability. Chuck Norris, the first fighting superstar, combined his notable kicking finesse with equally effective punching ability to create havoc on the tournament circuit.

While kicking ability is a must for sparring and self-defense, it's also quite important in *kata* or forms competition. Two of the great forms competitors from the 1980s, George Chung and John Chung (no relation), cite their skill in high kicking as key to their success. In modern karate competition, whether forms or sparring, superior kickers always gain attention and, more often than not, tournament victory as well.

Three important factors often cited by kicking experts are flexibility, knowledge of the mechanics of the kicks, and practice time spent perfecting each kick. Super kickers are willing to go beyond mere repetition, dedicating hours to their training.

A first step in developing kicking ability is to thoroughly understand each muscle group used in the performance of each kick. By recognizing the mechanical component of each kick, the practitioner may then be more aware of how to spend stretching time. In other words, if you can easily perform a front kick but have problems completing a side kick, then give priority to flexibility exercises involving the gluteal muscles when you stretch. Simply performing each kick with accurate technique is valuable, but to best enhance kicking ability kickers should also perform the flexibility exercises they need most.

Finally, remember that becoming a successful kicker might involve different challenges for different people. While some can naturally perform quality kicks, others may require additional work before attaining the level of expertise they desire. These variations are due to body build, limited practice time, or limited knowledge. Regardless of differences (but assuming the ability to perform kicking movements), you must understand the principles presented and relate them to your personal build. Use flexibility exercises to develop each kick. To become a super kicker, you'll have to spend plenty of time working on flexibility.

STRETCHING

Generally, reach-and-hold stretching (static stretching) is considered superior to bouncing or bobbing methods of stretching (ballistic stretching). Muscle tissue is elastic, and a greater amount of stretch is placed on a muscle in the held position. For example, if you stretch a muscle and hold it for 10 seconds, you get a full 10 seconds of stretch to lengthen the elastic fibers. On the other hand, 10 bouncing stretches cause a maximum stretch only during the end of each bounce, which lasts just a fraction of a second. The total stretch time you get in ballistic exercise is much less than you get in the reach-and-hold method.

Static stretching may also be advantageous in that it causes less muscle soreness and is less likely to cause tissue damage from sudden overstretching. In addition, static stretching does not evoke a reflex contraction of the stretched muscle. Ballistic stretching methods may cause a reflex contraction of the stretched muscle and reduce the amount of stretch that occurs.

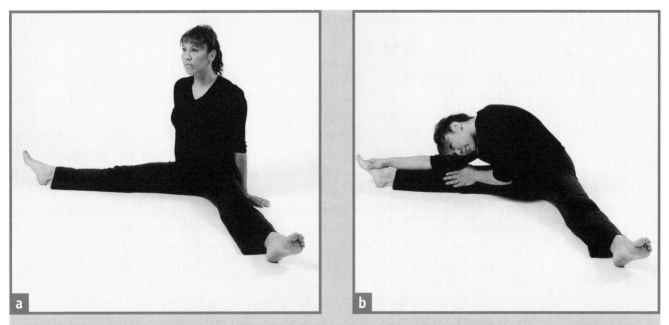

Most workouts begin with warm-up exercises and stretching. The static stretch (*a*), or reach and hold (*b*), techniques seem to work best for increasing flexibility.

Hold your static stretch positions for 10 to 60 seconds (the closer to 60, the faster you'll gain flexibility). You should do several sets of stretches for each workout, both before and after the workout.

The main muscles involved in sit-and-reach exercise include the hamstrings (biceps femoris, semitendinosus, and semimembranosus); the adductors (groin muscles including the adductor magnus, longus, brevis, and gracilis); and muscles of the spine, such as the internal and external obliques, erector spinae, and possibly the quadratus lumborum. The degree of muscular involvement changes with the position of the exercise. If the legs are relatively close together, the adductor muscles and oblique muscles (internal and external) are minimally stretched. When the legs are spread far apart, the adductors are stretched on the inside of the leg. This position is popular because it stretches several muscle groups at once. The major stretch of the oblique and quadratus lumborum muscles comes when the legs are spread and you lean over one of your legs, holding your head as close to the knee of that leg as possible. This puts more of a lateral stretch on the muscles on the opposite side of your body.

KICKING TECHNIQUES

The front, round, side, hook, and turning kicks are essential kicking skills for all forms of karate. Once you have mastered these moves, you can begin to experiment with style-specific modifications. Of all the kicking techniques, the front and round kicks deserve the most attention and hold the most potential for personal expression.

Front Thrust Kick

Most beginners in a karate class are taught the fundamentals of the front thrust kick during the first week of instruction. The front thrust kick is an excellent self-defense weapon because it is hard to block and easy to perform. The kick may be successfully used from either side, so it's quite adaptable to most situations. Some tournament competitors have abandoned the basic front kick in favor of the more flashy arcing kicks. However, the front thrust kick continues to be a stable part of any kicking arsenal.

Perform the front thrust kick with the back foot. With your left foot forward, kick with your right (reverse) foot. Perform the kick with your foot in a vertical position, delivering the kick on the line of attack to the point of impact. The contact area is the ball of the foot. Your foot then returns on the line of attack.

While performing the kick, keep your body in a vertical position, as leaning back might offset balance. As is true for any kicking technique, balance is jeopardized by removing your foot from the floor. It's essential that your

Front thrust kick. Proper execution of the front thrust kick includes a chambered position to raise the knee to the preferred height (*a*), and the leg extension (*b*). The contact surface is the ball of the foot. When the defender is wearing shoes, the tip of the toes can be used.

foot be retrieved from the target and returned to the floor as quickly as possible. The knee of your kicking leg is chambered at least at waist height.

To help maintain balance, try pushing your hips forward and slightly bending your support knee. This process, often used in the shotokan style, also dramatically increases power. When applied successfully, it's a very powerful kick. Your front foot (support foot) may pivot outward to permit the hip to be fully lifted for maximum penetration. This technique extends the distance in which contact can be made, adding to the deceptive quality of the front thrust kick.

The obvious problem with the front thrust kick is the risk of damaging your toes on contact. Keep your toes pulled back and make contact with the ball or bottom of the foot. If you're wearing heavy shoes, you might be able to hit with the toe of the shoe for a strong, penetrating effect.

The perfect front kick is displayed in this 1960s photo.

Front Snap Kick

The front snap kick is performed with the front foot from a fighting position. Typically, the foot is thrown forward for low kicks. Raising your knee to chamber the foot is required for strikes above the groin. The technique originates on the line of attack and, after impact, is quickly snapped back to the floor to avoid the possibility of the opponent catching or holding the kick. Like the front thrust kick, this kick is sometimes avoided because there's a risk of injuring your toes.

To complete the front snap kick, assume a fighting position. Chamber your knee at an appropriate height (which depends on the intended target), then extend your leg forward until contact is made. Using the front snapping method, experiment by kicking slightly inside or slightly outside the line of attack to the point of impact. This allows for different approaches in using the front snap kick.

The front snap kick is among the fastest of all kicks. In point competition, the target is generally the groin (when allowed). In self-defense, the target may include any part of the leg, groin, or stomach. Some karateka strike the groin with a variation of the front snap kick called a scoop kick, where the instep, rather than the ball of the foot, is the contact area.

Front snap kick. Typically used to initiate the attack or as a setup for subsequent attacks. The karateka initiates an unsophisticated chamber (*a*) and quickly snaps the kick out and back (*b*). Upper body movement is kept to a minimum.

Round Kick

The round kick is perhaps the most common kicking skill. It's both fast and defensively strong, an ideal choice for feeling out an opponent or scoring a point. When the contact area is the top of the instep, the round kick is considered primarily a tournament skill. The round kick can also be used effectively for self-defense, especially when you're wearing hard-soled shoes.

To perform the round kick, bring the knee and foot of your kicking leg up in a chambered position. Pivot your support-foot heel first in the direction of the kick to facilitate the twisting of your trunk for driving power. The contact area for the round kick is either the top of the instep or the ball of the foot. The foot travels in an arcing motion from outside the line of attack to the point of impact and returns on the same line of entry back to the chambered position and then to the floor.

Speed is essential when performing the round kick. Speed depends on your degree of flexibility, so stretch often. From a fighting stance, snap the

The round kick. Performed more often than any other kick in general karate practice. A chambered position is initiated (*a*) in order to complete one or more outward snapping techniques. The contact surface can be either the ball of the foot or the instep (*b*). The round kick is common to all styles but can differ in chamber position and contact surface. Be sure not to telegraph the round kick by emphasizing the chamber position.

round kick quickly to avoid permitting your opponent to catch the kick. Many competitors effectively use double or triple front-leg round kicks. To do so requires considerable practice and is associated with natural athletic ability and muscle control.

Experiment by skipping forward when completing the front-leg round kick to increase momentum, maintain balance, and extend the reach of the kick. The sliding or skipping motion performed with the support leg is complemented by the extension of the kicking leg naturally pulling the body forward.

Some karateka chamber the knee near chest level to complete kicks to the opponent's head. It's advisable to return the leg to the floor immediately after the round kick is completed, as having the knee chambered (a popular practice among Korean karate practitioners) may allow the opponent to rush in and score or knock the kicker off balance.

Reverse Leg Round Kick

The round kick is also effective when delivered from the reverse leg. By using the reverse-leg round kick you may increase power, but typically there's a trade-off in speed.

Be careful not to chamber your leg prematurely, thereby telegraphing the technique to the opponent. The reverse-leg round kick can be more easily detected than the front-leg round kick.

Many modern karate schools have adopted the Muay Thai method of performing the reverse-leg round kick. In the Thai boxing method, the support leg is used to quickly pivot—sometimes lifting slightly off the floor—and the contact surface is the top of the ankle or shin. When you deliver a Thai-style kick to an opponent's thigh, you generate tremendous energy, often knocking your opponent off balance or preventing him or her from advancing.

Reverse leg round kick. By chambering the round kick with the back leg, the karateka can increase power as the foot travels added distance to the target. The leg is first chambered (*a*), then extended in an arc toward the target (*b*). The contact surface can be the instep of the ball of the foot. Many fighters prefer to strike with the top of the shin when using this kick. The fighter becomes more open to counterattack by initiating the attack from the back side.

Side Kick

The side kick may be the most powerful kick in karate. From a fighting stance, chamber your kick high and keep your foot slightly inside or on the line of attack. As you thrust the kick forward, pivot the heel of your support leg in the direction of the kick. This action permits a full thrusting of the kick, thus increasing the pay load.

The contact area is the side of the foot or the bottom of the heel. The side of the foot often yields better penetration, whereas the bottom of the foot results in improved shock value. The power of the side kick can be increased by stepping into the kick. Take a step forward with your front foot (your kicking foot), then step or slide your reverse foot up to or behind (not in front of) the kicking leg. Then chamber the side kick and, using the momentum gained by stepping, follow through with a thrusting side kick.

The stepping side kick can easily knock opponents off balance or stop them in their tracks. In the 1960s, karate champion Joe Lewis often used the stepping side kick in competition. Lewis would appear to be stomping the

Side kick. Utilizes a chamber position that allows the kick to travel on the line of attack to the point of impact (*a*) and then be retrieved quickly in a similar motion. The contact surface can be either the side of the foot or the bottom of the heel (*b*). The side, round, and front kicks are typically the most practiced and most often used karate kicks. In each case, it is important to be non-telegraphic in delivery of the kicks.

ground with his front foot while getting prepared to lift off for the kick. His opponents could see it coming but were unable to stop the heavyweight athlete. On many occasions Lewis aimed his thrusting side kick at the opponent's hip, making severe contact. The opponent was shaken by the power of the kick (even though the match was supposedly noncontact), and in many cases his opponent was unable to kick until the soreness subsided. After effectively immobilizing an opponent, Lewis could score with a back fist. The next time the opponent saw Lewis stomp the floor he instinctively retreated, providing enough distance for Lewis to score again.

In self-defense the side kick offers terrific power and penetration. Practice the side kick by striking a heavy bag. There are many ways to perform the side kick, so experiment to discover what works best for you.

Hook Kick

Legendary karate kicker Bill Wallace chambers the side, hook, and round kicks in the same position. Opponents found it almost impossible to predict which kick would be delivered until it was too late to defend. The hook kick is performed much like a misdirected side kick that seems to miss the target and is then whipped back for a second chance to connect.

Assume the fighting position. Chamber the knee very high. Extend your leg outward in front of the target and snap the heel of your foot back and into the target. The contact area is the back of the heel.

The hook kick is difficult to perform if you're not very flexible. The primary target area is the head. Typically, the hook is used in combination with the round kick or side kick. If you and your opponent are on unmatched sides (for example, you are in right lead and he or she has a left lead), a good choice would be a fake round kick followed by a hook kick to the face.

The hook kick can also be used when you and your opponent are on matched sides. A fake side kick often brings his or her hand down, setting up a hook kick to the head. Usually, the hook kick combination requires a skipping or sliding pivot from the support foot for both balance and distance. Another popular combination from matched sides requires you to use the hook kick to reach out and pull your opponent's forward hand down, clearing the path for an immediate round kick to the face.

The hook kick is difficult to master but is very useful for combinations in point competitions.

Inside Kick

The inside kick is a popular little kick easily mastered by some yet never fully grasped by others. From the fighting position, raise your front foot as if you're seated and have begun to cross your legs in a "figure four" formation. The kicking leg is brought up 45 degrees inside the line of attack and, like a

Inside kick. Used when targets for the round and front kicks are not accessible, which occurs when opponents line up on unmatched sides. A brief, non-telegraphic chamber (a) is followed by a snapping kick that makes contact with the ball of the foot (b), or the instep when aimed at the head.

hook kick with your foot reversed, travels inside the line of attack to the point of impact and returns in the same line inside the line of attack and back to the floor.

The inside kick is used like a whip; the contact area is the ball of the foot, the instep, or the toes. Point competitors often use the inside kick for incredibly quick groin strikes. The groin strike would be even more effective in self-defense where hard contact is made. Full-contact fighters can use the inside kick with the instep whenever an opponent bends forward to avoid a punching combination.

Use an inside kick with a skipping step or by incorporating hip action or thrusting to increase the striking distance, deceptive quality, and momentum of your kick. A combination of a front snap kick, angling (45 degrees) round kick, and an inside kick might prove useful.

Instead of a 45-degree inside kick, some very flexible fighters can deliver a 90-degree inside kick effectively. Practice using a heavy bag. Attempt to lift your foot off the floor, strike the bag, and place your foot back on the floor all in one swift movement. The inside kick is very deceptive and, assuming it works for you, is a valuable part of the kicking arsenal.

When properly applied, the inside kick can be devastating.

Ax Kick

The ax kick gets its name from its ax-like precision. Until the 1970s, the ax kick was almost completely the domain of Korean karate stylists. As more karateka from different styles witnessed the effectiveness of the ax kick through competition, the technique was adopted by many who sought to improve their kicking repertoire.

To perform the ax kick, assume the fighting position. Point your kicking knee 45 degrees inside the line of attack. Raise the heel of your kicking leg straight up as if to sweep over the intended target. Then swiftly snap the heel of your kicking foot straight down through the target. Retract your foot at the last opportunity before striking the floor.

Like many kicks, the ax kick requires a high level of flexibility. Imagine reaching straight out and smashing your hand straight down on the top of someone's head. The ax kick is the same motion except that you hit with the back of your heel. Although it's possible to simply pick up your front foot as your opponent enters your critical space and drop the ax kick straight on top of him or her, the kick is most often performed with a skip or slide step. The step-first ax kick has greater momentum and distance.

The ax kick is chambered high (*a*) as the kicking leg is swung over the intended target (*b*) in order to strike with the heel in a sharp downward position.

Former Professional Karate Association (PKA) karate champ Jeff Smith, a practitioner of Korean karate, enjoyed great success by using the ax kick to knock down his opponent's forward blocking arm, creating an opening for a reverse punch or a round kick combination. From a fighting position, practice advancing your front foot forward, then quickly sliding your reverse foot up to the position of your front foot. Chamber the ax kick and complete the technique, striking your opponent's head for a point. If you miss, try to pull his or her guard down and follow up with a reverse punch.

Practice the ax kick on a heavy bag by cutting down diagonally across the upper part of the bag at head level. The ax kick is designed to "ax" the head, so train for flexibility. Although the ax kick often is used from the front side, the kick may be even more devastating when applied from the reverse leg. In so doing, you will increase both momentum and distance. The ax kick is not preferred by many styles, but when mastered it's a potent kick in any competition.

The ax kick finds its mark in this 1970s full-contact karate match.

Back Kick

Of the skills so far discussed, the back kick is the first to incorporate the added advantage of a spin. If you're in a left lead fighting stance, with your left foot in front, you will actually kick with your right leg by turning 180 degrees to your target.

Assume a fighting position. If you're right-side dominant, take a left lead stance, as this permits you to use your strong side for your turning back kick. With your left side in front, turn your head quickly in the direction of your right shoulder. In the same instant, chamber your right leg with the ball of the foot still on the floor by sliding your right leg up to your left leg. At this point, your eyes will have made contact with the intended target. Raise your right leg and strike the target. The contact area for the turning back kick is the bottom of the heel.

The turning back kick utilizes a simple chamber and is directed up to the target on the line of attack. The contact surface is the bottom of the heel.

Turning back kick. In some cases, the best option is to turn (*a*) in order to disguise the attack (*b*).

When the kick is completed you'll change from a left lead to a right lead stance. Don't attempt to make a 360-degree turn. To do so means you have missed your target. While some karateka practice turning 360 degrees for the back kick, there's nothing to be gained by this method since the focus of power is designed for a straight line.

Spinning Kicks

The spinning back kick is very deceptive. A useful combination might include striking your opponent hard with a spinning back kick, then pushing off the target to return to your original left lead stance. As you push off (the momentum of your retracting leg turns you in place of an actual push-off), prepare a left spinning back fist and complete the left back fist at the same time you complete your left lead stance. In effect, you kick low with the turning back kick, then hit high with a left spinning back fist.

Practice this routine against a heavy bag. As you perform the spinning back kick, you'll find that if you chamber for a side kick as you turn, you can complete a spinning side kick using the same entry.

Spinning side kick. This adds the variables of disguise and momentum to the basic kick (*a*). By spinning quickly, (*b*) the opponent often is unable to recognize the attacking weapon which has been supercharged (*c*) by the increased power of the body-shifting technique (*d*). The contact surface is the same as the basic side kick: you simply add the spin for power. Be aware that any time you take your eyes off of your target, you increase the potential for missing the opening.

When you master the spinning back and side kicks, you'll find that the spinning hook kick, spinning ax kick, and spinning crescent kick are all performed essentially the same way. The primary difference takes place in the chamber position for each kick.

To complete the spinning hook kick, follow the same guidelines for the spinning back kick. As you turn, chamber your leg high for the hook kick. In most cases you'll find that the momentum achieved with the spinning hook kick is best directed in a circle. Unlike the spinning back kick, in which power is focused in a straight line, the spinning hook kick can be practiced by making a complete 360-degree spin. If you do connect with the spinning hook kick, you'll stop with a 180-degree turn. If you miss, it often is effective to continue spinning back to your original position.

The spinning hook kick is most often employed while advancing toward an opponent. Because you must turn, the kick is easily telegraphed. For that reason, it's hard to connect with a spinning hook kick when thrown as a single direct attack. An effective way to disguise the spinning hook kick is to

Spinning hook kick. A sophisticated technique that, like most spinning kicks, has a very limited window of opportunity. The kick is best used in a combination attack. To complete the spinning hook kick, chamber the kick high (a) and let the momentum of the spin (b) deliver the pay load to the target, which is almost exclusively the opponent's head.

Spinning ax kick. Like the spinning hook kick, this is difficult to perform with a high degree of precision. Ideally, the kick should strike the top of the opponent's head, effecting a point or knockout. More often, the spinning ax kick is used simply to confuse the opponent with no real opportunity to score. On occasion, the ax kick strikes the opponent's arms, pulling them down and allowing the fighter to score with a reverse punch.

initiate a reverse round kick or a reverse front kick. As soon as the kick is completed, quickly perform the spinning hook kick. The reverse round kick to spinning hook kick combination might be very effective against an opponent who typically retreats from initial attacks to gain a better position for a counterstrike.

Because the spinning technique is used for the hook, side, ax, and crescent (inside) kicks, the fighter may quickly change from one technique to another. For example, a spinning side kick can easily be turned into a spinning hook kick if the opportunity arises. Similarly, the spinning hook kick can effectively be converted into a spinning ax kick.

The spin kicks are often used in tournament competitions but seldom employed effectively in no-holds-barred fighting. It would be unwise to recommend that the reader practice spinning kicks with the intent of knocking out an attacker in a street fight.

Kicking is an important element in developing a karate system. To become an expert with the kicks, you need to develop the attributes necessary for kicking, particularly flexibility. It's possible for some to have little or no difficulty with any kick, while others forever struggle with any kick other than the front kick. In most cases, if you put in the time, you can make kicks work for you.

Blocks and Traps

Blocks are perhaps the most misunderstood techniques in karate. In some classical styles there are more than two dozen types of fixed blocks. A nonclassical style may have only three to four set blocking techniques. I remember asking a sensei why I should not just move out of the way, or duck and attack. His response was that boxers duck and move out of the way; karateka block!

Classical karate does not teach you only to move out of the way. To stop an attack, you must block. As far back as the early 1970s, some instructors began promoting the idea that Asian sensei had hidden deadly strikes within their kata. The Asian masters refused to teach the deadly strikes (sometimes called *dim mak* or *tuite*) to non-Asians. While Americans were taught that a particular block was a defensive motion, others were taught that what appeared to be a block to the uninformed person was actually a strike or a grappling method. Perhaps this explains why there are so many blocks in classical karate and why some of them seem to have no useful purpose.

BLOCKING

In the art and sport of karate, the practice of blocking has been used over the years in three distinct ways:

1. A way to stop or redirect your opponent's strikes. Be advised that this may or may not be an effective way to use blocks.

Tournament champion John Worley immobilizes his opponent by grabbing the gi and preparing for a reverse punch. Referee Chuck Norris prepares to call the point in the 1960s photo.

2. A method of limb destruction to immobilize an attack by striking your opponent's weapon with force.

3. A facade to disguise a pressure-point attack or your attempt to grapple an opponent's limbs. There is little if any published material that provides conclusive evidence about how these techniques were developed.

Traditional systems for blocking suggest that the block is most often used to stop or redirect an attack. Today, the idea of assuming a wide, deep stance, pulling one hand back to the hip, and using your other hand to stop a strike seems outdated—and it should be. Those who practice blocking as a form of limb destruction or grappling would agree.

Okinawan karate master Seiyu Oyata was perhaps the first person to introduce the theory of tuite—using strikes to specific areas of the body in order to achieve a knockout with little effort—throughout the United States. As early as 1981, Grand Master Oyata traveled extensively, introducing karate instructors to grappling techniques hidden in the kata. Some of these seminar attendees became personal students and continued to teach this innovative approach to blocking and striking. Others created their own interpretations or emphasized the idea that a block was intended for limb destruction. Of the three interpretations, perhaps the most practical approach is that blocking is a means of limb destruction.

As beginners, most karateka have inadvertently experienced the effects of limb destruction. A front kick that makes heavy contact with the opponent's elbow, a round kick that strikes the opponent's raised knee, or a hook that gets caught by the biceps all are examples of limb destruction, albeit unintended.

Follow these suggestions for effective limb destruction:

- Against a side kick, attempt to catch the kick between your elbow (coming down on the ankle) and your knee (being raised up to strike any part of the foot, ankle, or leg).

- Strike a front kick with your elbow, or, if you have strong fists, catch the front kick with a back fist. Strong-fisted fighters can literally punch the leg of an opponent as he or she tries to deliver a front kick.

- Against a round kick, keep both arms up and pull the kick down into your raised knee, striking the sensitive area inside your opponent's shin.

- Against a jab, time it so that you raise your elbow just as your opponent's fist gets close to your face.

- Against a slow hook or an extended arm, throw your own hook punch, striking your opponent's biceps, immobilizing his or her arm.

Classic Blocking

Classical karate systems often employ a wide, deep stance (front balance) in which the legs are positioned apart as much as one and a half times the width of the shoulders. The front foot faces forward, with the front knee

Karate blocks may have different interpretations depending on the style. While most systems teach blocks as defensive strikes (*a-c*), other styles interpret blocks as types of limb destruction (*d*) to be used against strikes and kicks. In this interpretation, the block is actually a strike, or the block may be performed instantaneously with the strike (*e-f*).

bent 90 degrees. The back foot is turned outward 45 degrees, and the back leg is straight. Both feet are flat on the floor in this stance.

To complete the low block, the karateka slides the back foot forward in what is called a C or crescent step. In crescent stepping, the back foot is brought up near the front foot, then out to assume the wide, deep stance. While stepping, the blocking arm is chambered in front of the body. As body weight shifts forward, the block is extended. The opposite arm is brought back to the corresponding hip as the blocking arm extension is completed.

The classical block. To perform the classical low block, begin from the chambered position (*a*), then extend the arms downward (*b*). The high block (*c*) and the X-block (*d*) are used in most classical styles.

In this classical interpretation, the head is left unguarded. The body is fully exposed. The deep stance leaves the karateka unable to quickly reposition. If the technique is used as a block, it leaves the practitioner far too vulnerable. Intending the block for limb destruction makes sense, and thinking not about blocking but about how the opponent will be pulled in and struck is perhaps even a better way to approach what has been called a classic block.

Nonclassical Blocking

Bruce Lee once took out his wallet and threw it to a friend. The friend simply put up his hand to block it. Lee asked him, "What method did you use?" The friend replied that he had no method—he simply responded. For many beginners, learning classical blocks seems like a bad idea. The stance is deep and awkward. Moving from one position to the next is difficult. Unless the sensei has a very convincing reason why you must move like this, classical blocking will be the most unpopular techniques in the curriculum. It is also hard to use classical blocks in real self-defense. As a result, nonclassical blocking methods are developed to reflect the needs of individual fighters.

For the most part, blocking is a natural response. Demanding that there's only one way to perform a block is to forfeit its spontaneity. Here are some blocking guidelines:

- After you complete a block, swiftly pull your arm back to guard your upper body.
- When it's effective, do not block but strike your opponent's limb.
- If you extend a block and leave it out, attempt to grab or immobilize your opponent's limb.
- Follow a block with a strike, or reposition yourself.
- When possible, avoid blocking and move out of the line of fire.
- Attempt to parry or redirect while you reposition.

TRAPPING

In trapping, you momentarily immobilize your opponent's limb. Trapping is not an end in itself but a method for safely bridging a gap, a technique for rhythm disruption, or an efficient way to clear an obstruction to gain access to a target. Trapping employs the hands and arms as well as the feet for lower-body traps.

Trapping is sometimes confused with checking. Checking is a way to gauge distance, in which a hand is extended in a slap-like manner to check the position of your opponent's limbs. American kenpo founder Ed Parker was a master of checking. His lightning quick checks were evidenced by what was heard as a rapid tapping sound. The merits of rapid checking are debatable.

In contrast to the classical styles, the modern American interpretations originate from a fighting position (*a*) and have deleted a strong chamber position. The blocks are thrown out much like strikes. The low block (*b*), middle block (*c*), and high block (*d*) are quick and efficient. In most cases, a good blocking system can be found by using the most effective concepts of the classical and modern styles.

Perhaps a better choice for many fighters, trapping not only stops the opponent's strike, but temporarily immobilizes the opponent's offense allowing the fighter to execute a technique to an unprotected target. In this sequence, the fighter intercepts the opponent's strike (*a-b*), then traps the opponent's striking arm (*c*) which permits a successful strike to an unprotected target (*d*). Additional trap/strike combinations also are available. Here, the author immobilizes the arm (*e*), thereby setting up a final strike (*f*).

Trapping is similar to the boxing technique of parrying. To parry is to quickly redirect a fist by what appears to be a short, swift slap. Trapping is catching the limb for a second while delivering a counterstrike. Trapping allows for better access to a target and improves your accuracy since the target has limited movement. Here are some useful trapping skills:

- Using a technique that ranks somewhere between a palm heel strike and an open-hand slap, pin your opponent's arm against his or her body. Do not grab and hold the arm. The objective is to temporarily immobilize the arm so that the path is cleared to the target (the head).

- If your opponent blocks your back-fist strike, trap his or her blocking arm at the elbow. When the block is cleared, strike!

- If your opponent raises his or her hands in a boxing stance, trap the forward arm, temporarily rendering the arm useless, and strike.

- Using a cupped hand, trap and pull your opponent off balance by trapping his or her forward arm.

- Trap your opponent's leg by placing your foot against his or her leg, blocking or checking any attempted kick.

- Step on your opponent's foot to immobilize the leg and effectively abbreviate any advancement. Be prepared to use hand strikes.

- Double up on traps to arms. Use trapping to bridge forward and advance your attack. The result is not to trap but to safely gain access to a target and improve accuracy through temporary immobilization.

I remember taking a class years ago from a classically trained Korean karate master. He carried a short stick and each time a student deviated from what the master envisioned as the perfect technique, the student would receive a quick smack with the stick. The block had to be performed only one way.

In 1960s karate competition, trapping or immobilizing was demonstrated most often as simply holding or grabbing. The author demonstrates that by grabbing the opponent's sleeve he can more easily strike the opponent's body with a reverse punch (*a*) or a side kick (*b*).

You could hear him walking up and down the floor, smacking students with the stick.

It occurred to me that the master's way of performing his blocks was never going to be my way of performing the blocks; therefore, I received quite a few smacks. At the time I was glad to receive the master's attention, but the lesson that I learned was that perfection is seldom achieved.

If you are able to block a punch or kick, be satisfied. Don't worry about whether or not it was a perfect block. It is more important to set footwork (mobility), punches, kicks, and strategy as priorities for your training. Classical blocks are for fighters who can't move.

Karate for Self-Defense

Self-defense might be more about mentality than physicality. As humans we are blessed with a complex network of nerves called the autonomic nervous system. Thousands of years ago our ancestors relied on immediate adrenaline rushes to avoid being eaten by predators. Today, books have been written about the negative effects of adrenaline to the body, and drugs have been prescribed to curb its influence on our health and actions.

We can feel its effect in the form of increased heart rate, cardiac output, breathing rate, blood pressure. According to cardiologist Dr. James O'Keefe, activation of what is called the sympathetic nervous system sets off an exhilarating adrenaline rush which assists the body in response to threat and readies us to flee or fight (assuming that we are in imminent danger of a predatory attack). The problem is that this same adrenaline rush can cause us to be immobilized if we fail to flee or must call on our mental ability to negotiate a peaceful conclusion to an altercation rather than rely on our physical strength.

In a sort of yin/yang relationship, an opposing measure called the parasympathetic nervous system calms us down. A *New York Times* syndicated article on health indicated that, by forming strong social connections, such as marriage and religious faith, we can curb an overactive sympathetic system. Membership in a karate school can help form strong social bonds. Success in karate training can promote faith in our ability to survive. The realization that we will not be harmed can serve to activate the parasympathetic nervous system. In a real fight we want to activate the parasympathetic nervous system.

When taught by a highly skilled, disciplined instructor in an environment that nurtures the complex social group configurations required for maturity in the activity, traditional karate could well be the most effective form of self-defense training ever developed for large-scale application, but not because karate teaches us a better way to fight. For the advanced practitioner karate can activate a state of *mushin*, a calm and relaxed mind, which will have the effect of supercharging the parasympathetic nervous system. Perhaps this is what happens to zen masters who put their hands into boiling water, or to survivors of death-defying encounters. They have faith and a clear mental image that they will succeed. Experts agree that in real-life scenarios, physical skills are of secondary importance. The person who wins the fight wins as a direct result of successful psychological preparation, which enables him or her to establish and maintain a mental advantage throughout the confrontation. An enraged man with a pocket knife has been known to control an entire office of employees even though, acting as a group, the employees could easily overpower him. What you mentally take into an altercation makes all the difference.

A popular view held by nontraditionalists is that the predator-prey scenario is the ultimate test of the validity of martial arts. Many experts in the predator-prey philosophy—including some highly trained and persuasive people—suggest that we would be well advised to abandon classical training for fear that at any moment we could fall into a life-and-death struggle with a maniac on drugs. In such situations, nontraditionalists believe traditional karate is of little use, and they have effectively persuaded many that they are right.

Against the air choke, the defender places her chin down (*a*) to lessen the effects of the choke. By twisting back or under (*b-c*), she negates the air choke, then escapes (*d*). Efficient techniques are exclusive to no single style of karate but reflect the positive aspects of all styles.

But the predator-prey scenario—that highly skilled predators want to attack us—makes up only a small part of self-defense. The vast majority of self-defense situations develop as a result of a stimulus and a response. A person creates—through gestures, words, physical contact, or other forms of body language—a stimulus that elicits an aggressive response. This response, though usually verbal, is sometimes physical. Through his or her own choices and actions, a person initiates self-defense.

Most self-defense situations can be effectively controlled through nonviolent means, including diffusion, de-escalation, and retreat from the scene. Unfortunately, it's possible for someone to get so fixated on a single possibility (e.g., the predator-prey scenario) that he or she misses an overwhelming majority of the benefits that karate training has to offer.

If your chosen lifestyle is such that you simply must frequent the proverbial biker bar; dine or shop in a high crime district; or associate with known gang members, criminals, drug dealers, and other predator types, then you certainly are advised to discover the most effective short-term form of self-defense. Depending on how much time you have to train, traditional karate might or might not be your best choice. To reap the benefits of classical karate, you must invest time and self-discipline.

THE TRADITIONAL APPROACH

Traditional karate is designed to improve character, develop confidence to meet life's challenges, and achieve goals. According to Chuck Norris, perhaps the world's best-known master of the empty hand, "Karate means developing yourself as a person. It involves developing respect for yourself, which in turn instills respect for others. What I stress is that [students have] a clear mental image of what they want, the desire to achieve it, the determination and patience to stay the course, and the discipline to study and train accordingly. If you follow this formula and your goal is within your range of accomplishment, then success will be yours."

The time-tested emphasis on traditional karate instruction is on the long-range goals of improving or changing the participant's character to reflect the goals of martial arts—virtuous conduct in the face of hardship or combat. The prudent karateka should investigate different methods of physical training, so long as each method selected yields the benefits of a successful socialization process culminating in a psychological perspective that recognizes the importance of the individual. Acquired self-efficacy and self-esteem, by-products of an organized karate school, have more utility than sheer brutal force when it comes to avoiding trouble and controlling a self-defense scenario.

As a karateka progresses through a highly regimented ranking structure, roles requiring disciplined behavioral patterns are established. The yellow-belt student observes the actions of the green-belt student. Perhaps imagining themselves in the superior role, yellow-belt students might inadvertently practice the proper pattern of behavior required of a superior rank. The yellow-belt student takes on the role of his or her superior and is psychologically tested with the same prescribed duties and expectations as if he or she actually holds the higher status. In so doing, the yellow belt prepares to assume the green-belt rank. The same can be said of the green belt desiring to advance to the brown belt.

The process of socialization required for each rank prepares students to achieve virtuous conduct, as failure to observe rules or expected forms of behavior at any level can result in expulsion from the group, demotion, or other forms of discipline used to steer students toward acceptable action. This perspective recognizes that established patterns of group life are propagated through interaction through which generalized symbols (rank, belts, uniforms, etc.) and modes of interpretation are commonly exchanged, often through the completion of organized activities.

Each time students observe how their superiors interact with others, their own opinions of proper behavior are influenced. Through such interaction, individuals in the dojo acquire a cognitive understanding of existent norms that mandate responsible and acceptable forms of behavior. Through participation in kata, kumite, and so on, common expressions and values are shared, wherein participants dramatize their roles in ways that best benefit each situation. Through their actions, students lay claim to their understanding of reality.

Three to four years of continuous training in the dojo with appointed advancements in status can greatly influence how a person acts in a threatening situation. If the process has been successful, the karateka will act with virtuous conduct regardless of the outcome of the event. Often, black-belt experts, though possessing the potential to inflict great harm, choose not to use their power. Realizing that their strike could result in the death of an attacker, they opt to turn the other cheek and walk away.

To someone not tempered by years of training in the traditional dojo, walking away from a fight might be viewed as cowardice. In fact, such behavior reflects a higher state of human understanding: how to accept a subordinate position in order to maintain a superior's position. This unique understanding is produced in part during symbolically violent training in which a karateka is expected to fantasize taking the life of his or her partner. In creating the act of justifiable murder, the karateka must evoke controlled rage and perhaps hatred. Like a vaccine, emotions are evoked to allow the karateka to develop control of each thought preceding the emotion. Since the mind does not distinguish the real situation from the imagined, the emotions become real.

Sport psychologists have maintained that when participants engage in what is called "vivid imagery" (the type frequently produced in one-step sparring) and completely absorb themselves in the activity, the brain interprets the images as identical to reality-based interactions. Adding to the validity of the situation are stress-producing factors, including the expectations of others who are watching, and the skill, appearance, and reputation of the opponent.

In a variation of the grab from behind, the karateka utilizes the elbow strike to escape. The elbow may be used to strike the stomach or groin, or the hand may be employed to strike the groin.

At once the opponent can become a trusted friend or a vicious opponent bent on killing. Psychotherapist Mark Vloskey, PhD, maintains that within the context of a single exercise, the karateka can sample the emotions of respect, hate, fear, remorse, and mercy.

On any given night in the dojo, the karateka recognizes extreme stress and emotional bliss. He has killed, and he has trusted his life to others. He has shared remorse, joy, and friendship. In his mind, he has recorded the emotions as real—he actually felt, controlled, and released each emotion. He has prepared himself for more meaningful interpersonal communication and relationships. Thus, processes have taken place at different levels over a period of years as the socialization in the dojo has been completed. Is the student capable of self-defense? Yes.

Through training, students develop the ability to role play. Through vivid imagery, they automatically begin to play out confrontations. In their mind, they see the fight escalating. They strike their opponent, causing great damage. They feel remorse. They feel pity for the injured attacker. In a merciful gesture, they choose to diffuse the argument or to walk away. They view fighting as an honorable exercise and choose not to dishonor their training by engaging in an avoidable incident. Aggression is, after all, a learned response. We become aggressive by observing parents, teachers, and other role models and then imitating them. Aggression is the result of rewards and the systems of punishment to which the individual has been exposed. The traditional karate dojo treats aggression in a strict matter-of-fact manner. Aggression is controllable, an available option when needed but deplorable when uncontrolled.

THE NONCLASSICAL APPROACH

Is there a need for nonclassical karate for self-defense? Of the thousands of people who enter karate schools, less than 10 percent earn the black-belt rank. It's at the black-belt level that the aforementioned emotional control is best expressed. In fact, some traditionalists claim that earning the first-degree black belt merely indicates the student is ready to learn the art. As a result of so many people beginning to study classical karate only to quit after a few years, a nonclassical approach has been developed.

Nonclassical karate received much support from the philosophy of Bruce Lee in the 1960s. Modern nonclassical karate emphasizes the "anything goes" aspect of mixed martial arts training. For the most part, the sense of virtuous duty valued by traditionalists is abandoned. In its place are intricate drills intended to reproduce street conditions and short-term advantages for those unable to take the longer path to virtuous conduct.

Some entrepreneurial self-defense "experts" have dismissed the use of karate in self-defense. Make no mistake: karate is a most efficient means of self-defense. However, to experience the "empty mind/hand" of karate, years of training are required. Sometimes the time-conscious American wants a faster method. Is there a way to maintain karate and adapt the physical skills to realize functional levels in less time than usual?

The attacker employs a grab to the throat (*a*). The defender weaves her hands through the assailant's outstretched arms to break free (*b*). Stepping away and out of the attacker's line of fire (*c*), the defender utilizes an elbow strike and follows with a grab to the neck and a knee to the face (*d-f*). Simple techniques like the elbow and knee defenses often present an appropriate window of opportunity. More sophisticated skills reflecting unique aspects of a classical art are, in many cases, inappropriate in the complexities of the combat arena.

RESPONSE TO AN ATTACK

Several changes quickly occur when you're about to be attacked. Your brain is bombarded with urgency and uncertainty. *Will I be hurt? Will I be able to respond?* Your brain searches for corresponding data to answer its questions. *Has this ever happened to me before? If so, how did I handle it?* Your brain searches for more information. A decision must be made fast. *If I'm injured, what will people think and do?*

The attacker moves in close, a grin on his face. He smells of alcohol. He's dirty. He's loud and vulgar. What to do? Your first instinct is to hide, deny that this is happening. So many thoughts! Your heart pounds fast. You feel chest pain. Your legs feel paralyzed. There's no strength in your arms.

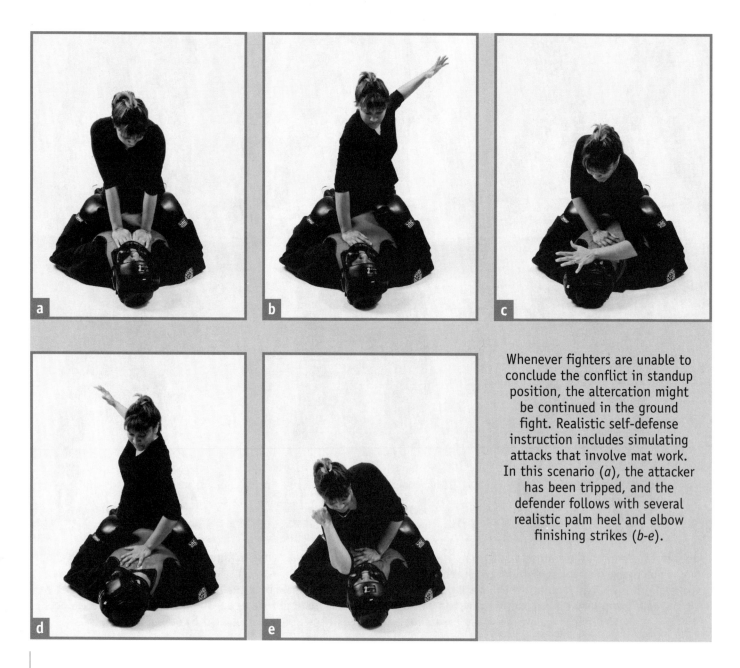

Whenever fighters are unable to conclude the conflict in standup position, the altercation might be continued in the ground fight. Realistic self-defense instruction includes simulating attacks that involve mat work. In this scenario (*a*), the attacker has been tripped, and the defender follows with several realistic palm heel and elbow finishing strikes (*b-e*).

Your throat tightens, making speech difficult. Finally, words come out. Negotiations begin. Your attacker demands money. *My wallet? Where is it? Should I go for it?* Suddenly you remember the picture of your kids in your wallet. *What if I'm killed here?* So many thoughts! Your attacker screams again. A gun is pressed tight against your temple. You have taken karate for six months. You know five kata, more than 50 techniques. Which should you use? In the dojo, you never faced this problem.

I can't kick because he's too close. Maybe I could use a block. But what if I miss? Hesitation . . . and then it's too late. The attacker has reached into your pocket and taken your wallet, and now he's gone. What now? You're okay. Should you call the police? There will be questions. *What could I have done? What should I have done? What will people think and say?*

For the small percentage of people who master karate as the art of the empty mind, the above scenario would not take place. They would simply hand over the money or perhaps respond if a weakness was observed. For those who, for whatever reason, elect not to follow the path of mushin and need immediate gratification in street combat, I suggest a more synergistic approach to seeking the confidence of self-defense.

SYNERGISTIC KARATE FOR SELF-DEFENSE

Self-defense is a competitive event in which two or more participants actualize a challenge for survival. The key to winning any competition is the successful combination of attributes, strategy, and chance. While we cannot program chance, much can be done to ensure success by developing strategy and certain attributes. By understanding the importance of these factors in winning, we can analyze any martial art and determine its potential success for the performer before any confrontation occurs.

When the art of karate was first introduced to North America in the late 1940s and 1950s, it quickly earned the reputation for being the most advanced method of self-defense ever developed. Times have changed. Because America became a melting pot for martial arts from many countries, fighters in the United States became more sophisticated in a variety of arts and fighting ranges.

Most karate systems introduced to the United States after World War II represented new dojo arts developed not on the battlefield but in the dojo. The elements of actual combat were replaced with a need for safety in training, resulting in a form of dramaturgical manipulation called kata. The strategy of kata is to fight an imaginary opponent. As much as 60 percent of all classical karate instruction focused on performance of kata. To demonstrate focus and power, the karateka typically broke boards, bricks, and other objects.

In many cases, the strategy for learning karate has been to reach mushin through prearranged combat and focused attacks on inanimate objects. While this system has proven effective for character development, it lacks the reality base needed for effective self-defense obtained in a short time. Some karateka who possess the right attributes of speed and power can effectively

Against the two-hand grab (*a*), the defender initiates a head butt and releases the attacker's grip (*b-c*). Sensing his vulnerability, she quickly follows with ear strikes (*d*). She then controls the neck (*e*) and completes a knee strike to the groin (*f*). Because all karate styles utilize these strikes, modern independent karate recognizes no boundaries in selecting the best response.

use even the most traditional karate skills. Others must adapt or supplement their practice methods to become more adept at street defense encounters. Here are some examples that show the importance of strategy and attributes.

After watching a professional basketball game, a spectator concludes that the best strategy to win the game is to maneuver close to the net then slam dunk the ball to score. It's a good plan, but the attributes of height and jumping

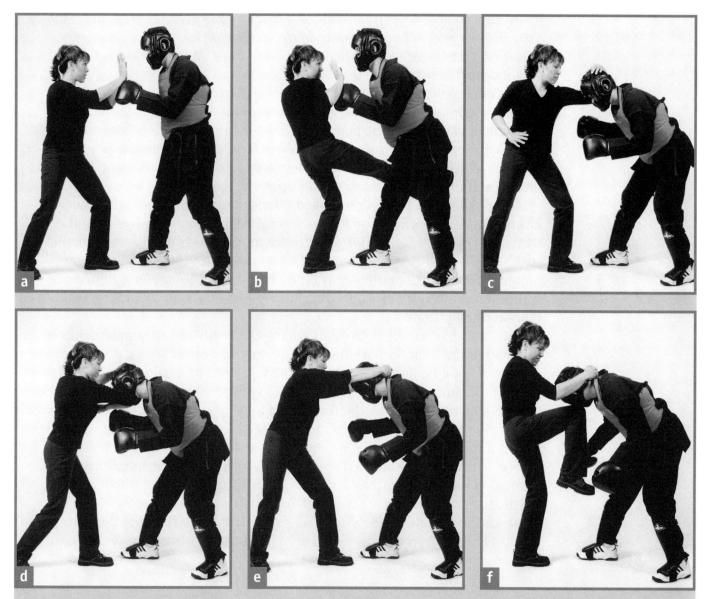

With the attacker in full body armor (*a*), a free form attack is experienced. To gain skill in more realistic self-defense, the defender performs with full contact. In the full-contact simulated attacks, the defender experiences a higher state of mental aggression while controlling the physical aspects of contact and increased heart rate. In this sequence the defender kicks to the groin (*b*), then controls the attacker's neck (*c-d*) to finish with a knee to the head (*e-f*).

power are mandatory in order for the strategy to work. If you are five feet, five inches tall, the slam dunk strategy will not work.

Imagine a 250-pound tough guy defeated by a frail young woman whose thumb to the eye is considered a superior strategy. The tough guy possessed the superior attributes—size and strength—yet the young woman in a frantic attempt to defend herself clawed at the attacker's eye and found success. Strategy can at times prevail over attributes.

Now let's imagine that the young woman decides that the thumb-to-the-eye strategy is unbeatable. When confronted by another thug, she simply waits until the right moment and then employs her strategy. This time, the thug smacks her in the head and knocks her unconscious. Her strategy, superior on one occasion, fails in the second attack. When strategy fails, attributes must prevail.

My concern is that the physical karate taught in many schools uses skills that have a limited window of opportunity. Many karate-style kicks, blocks, and punches are limited in application, like the thumb-to-the-eye technique. In actual combat, there's no opportunity to use the 30-some kicks and 40-some blocks and strikes found in a dozen or more kata. Too many choices often result in immobilization and improper responses.

Karate skills work best when applied at long range, sometimes called karate/kickboxing range, where the fighter has sufficient space to advance and retreat and get set to hit. Unfortunately for the karate-trained fighter, actual street combat almost always takes place in close proximity. At the distance required for karate, the fighter is best advised to negotiate and diffuse the confrontation. It is up close, in the clinch position, toe to toe, that physical reprisal often is required.

To be effective in self-defense, the karateka is advised to supplement his or her training by incorporating techniques from other styles. Techniques effective in boxing, jiujitsu, escrima, and so on can be easily adapted to the karate program. In other words, use what works, regardless of the style.

When fighting, consider the total effect to be greater than the sum of the effects independently. Abandon the misplaced tradition of limiting yourself to using only the skills of a specific style of karate. Ultimately, you must achieve success in matching a chosen strategy to your own personal attributes. Through a thorough synthesis of strategy and attributes, you might achieve a synergistic progression, a genesis of new potentials readily available for the karateka to apply in self-defense. The combination of achieving the path to mushin and modern eclectic skills based on strategy and attributes is a hard combination to defeat.

Competition
and Strategy

In previous chapters, I have maintained that all styles of karate represent a specific plan of action. This plan or strategy is reflected in the way you compete in the ring or in the street. Style is produced upon several variables, including your personal attributes, view of reality, preferred fighting range, preferred rules of fair play, and concept of what's required in combat. Understand these variables when determining the utility of the style, its applications to your needs, and whether it represents a system that is functional for you.

In many ways, all styles that originated in Japan represent the social values experienced in Japan. Traditional Japanese karate is considered very rigid in its concepts of fair play and combat. If you want to learn shotokan karate, for example, you're expected to adopt—at least to some degree—the world view of Gichin Funakoshi, the founder of shotokan. Funakoshi was an upstanding citizen of Japan and a highly respected educator who introduced karate to his public school system. He was not known to be a street fighter; rather, he was a man of superior character who lived for many years. He died honorably at age 89.

Representing a different view of combat, Bruce Lee claimed, at least during his youth, to be a street fighter. Lee's system used a multicultural, multiple-range concept. He was said to possess a charismatic, yet highly volatile, character. In part, his short life was a consequence of his lifestyle. He died by misadventure at age 32.

In developing your own plan, I advise you to position yourself somewhere between Funakoshi's character traits and Lee's concept of combat. In other words, the traditional social instruction system that Funakoshi represented can be maintained while incorporating the effective combat method used by Lee.

STRATEGY FOR COMPETITION

In the history and development of karate, physical skills and methods of execution have always varied. Most schools concentrate on technique execution and the development of attributes necessary to perform the techniques properly. The term "strategy" is often limited to the attempt to best execute the plan presented by the founder of the style. In both competition and self-defense, some karateka are restricted to focusing their attention on representing the style rather than winning in a simple, direct way.

The most often used strategy for competition is to change techniques. For example, when a fighter tries to score with a back fist and it does not work, he or she tries a different technique. The idea that using various techniques is the best strategy seems popular in karate circles, yet some of the best fighters of the 1960s and 1970s, including Bill Wallace and Joe Lewis, relied on few techniques. Wallace was best known for his round-hook–side-kick combination. Lewis established his reputation on effectively using the side kick and forward hand strike.

The number of techniques available is not as important as the way in which each technique is performed. In 40 years of karate competition, I have found three hand skills (the back fist, the hook, and the reverse punch) and three kicks (the front kick, the round kick, and the side kick) to be most effective. The best strategy for competing in the ring or on the street is to control your opponent by controlling your distance. Always try to be in a position that allows you to score but renders your opponent unable to return fire. One of the world's great military strategists, Sun Tzu, author of *The Art of War*, presented a strategy more than 2,500 years ago that remains effective today: "He will win who is prepared and waits for the unprepared enemy."

In his book titled *Boxing: A Self Instruction Manual*, author Edwin L. Haislet presented the concept of controlling the opponent so that he is unable to get set to hit. Much of Haislet's work was studied and taught by Bruce Lee. On his death, Lee's estate published the *Tao of Jeet Kune Do* in which Haislet's work was quoted more than any other source. Former fighter and now renowned seminar leader Joe Lewis has produced several videotapes focusing on the topic of set point control.

In 1989, I co-authored with Lewis an article for *Karate International* magazine. In the article, we noted that when offensively approaching an opponent, you must always seek to gain time and distance. Without these conditions in your favor, you will have no strategic advantage.

Properly executing techniques is the first level of developing a strategy for competition. The second level of development is learning to maneuver safely and effectively so that your approach (the way you bridge the gap between yourself and your opponent) is better than your opponent's approach.

Controlling the "get set to hit" strategy. The fighter on the right can be seen using an offensive strategy that does not allow the opponent to get set. When the opponent is unprepared to answer the attack, success is guaranteed.

For an opponent to deliver a strong offense, they must get set to strike. To "get set" means taking a balanced stance that provides the opportunity of delivering the best attack. Your goal is to keep them from getting set so that they are forced to retaliate from a position that dissipates strength, giving you the advantage.

To establish control of an opponent's set point, you must first establish position and then deliver a strong offense. In doing so, you keep your opponent busy while setting up your own attack. An example of this concept has been used in many old westerns and war movies. Whenever the "good guy" is penned in by an enemy, he tells his partner to "cover me" as he moves into a better position. By having his partner draw the enemy's attention, he becomes mobile and thus able to establish a position of greater strength to eventually neutralize the enemy's attack. Essentially, in karate, you move and strike in one position in order to set up a stronger or finishing blow.

The jab and the front or round kick are often used to establish position and discover your opponent's intention. The advanced fighter understands the potential repercussions of the lead hand or foot strike. For every strike, there is a response, often yielding an opening. Attack your opponent where he is weak, not strong.

Visualize how this strategy could work in self-defense. By kicking your opponent at the knee, you create a disturbance to the lower body, forcing him or her to focus on a low defense. This opens the upper body for an undefended attack. By neutralizing his upper body defense, your strategy results in a position of strength.

To be effective, you need a strong lead-off technique. The lead-off technique you select should give you time to mount a stronger follow-up and let you reposition to improve accuracy and power. A problem with many fighters is that they are so eager to initiate an attack that they end up striking from a point of weakness to a position of strength. A probing lead jab may have serious repercussions unless you reposition or follow up immediately with a strong technique. A strong lead-off technique takes away your opponent's balance, distance, and aim, causing him to hesitate mentally, perhaps allowing you to move out of the line of attack.

If an opponent is well anchored in a strong stance, they are in a position of strength, prepared to mount a strong attack or to answer your probing lead hand strike. You must either step out of the line of attack and reposition or cause your opponent to hesitate. As you reposition to a position of strength, your opponent also attempts to nullify your advantage by repositioning. Think of a verbal argument, when someone counters your address with their own retort. It also occurs in a simple shoving contest and in a predator-prey scenario (discussed in chapter 8). The "cat and mouse" position/reposition response is observable in nearly any kind of contest.

During the split second when your opponent hesitates to reestablish a defense/offense or reposition, you strike. You have neutralized your opponent and gained the advantage. You must follow up with superior fire power and reposition so that your position of strength is not diminished. Observe the old adage to "hit and move."

THREE TYPES OF DEFENSIVE FIGHTERS

Generally, fighters can be categorized as jammers, blockers, or runners. Jammers come right at you, like a bull in a china shop, preferring to jam your techniques, stay on you, and nullify your offense by not giving up space. This type of fighter respects superior fire power, which causes them to hesitate.

Blockers attempt to obstruct each attack, which opens them to fakes and feints, causing them to block or defend in the wrong position.

Runners react defensively by moving from attacks. A good fake sends them running. To overcome this type of fighter, you must have strong initial techniques or immobilize his or her position as you strike.

No matter which kind of defensive fighter you're up against, you have a choice of five methods for bridging the gap and offensively approaching him or her: a direct attack, an indirect attack, a combination attack, an immobilization attack, or a rhythm disruption attack. Let's look briefly at each of these.

Direct Attack

As the name implies, a direct attack is the simple execution of a technique. Some techniques, such as the jab and round kick, are perfectly suited for simple, direct attacks. Other more complex techniques, including spinning kicks and reverse hand strikes, are not so easily executed without some kind of set-up. The direct attack represents an initial movement. A simple, direct movement has a greater chance of being undetected when the variables of speed and power are proportionally increased.

Direct attack. In using this as a strategy for offensively approaching the opponent, simply strike the opponent. Here, the fighter (*a*) utilizes an inside kick (*b*) to strike an unprotected abdomen (*c*).

To practice the direct attack, take turns with a partner initiating simple kicks or punches. Notice how easily your partner blocks or repositions to avoid the strike. When he is off-balance or when your attack is quick or has enough power, a direct attack can be effective. All beginners are coached to use simple, direct attacks.

Indirect Attack

When a fake is used to set up a direct attack, you have an indirect attack. You may fake a kick or punch or move your upper or lower body to elicit a defensive response from your opponent. Most fighters quickly learn that if you fake a jab low, the opponent will often pull down his or her guard, opening a line for an unobstructed jab to the head.

One of the first techniques taught in Korean karate classes is to fake a low round kick and follow with a high round kick to score. Sometimes in a match an opponent will respond if you fake with a hip as though you intend to kick but instead use a forward hand strike to score.

Working with a partner, observe how much movement is required to cause them to react to a faked technique. If you fake a runner, expect him or her to quickly reposition out of the way. The best results for faking are when you're matched against a blocker, as he by nature blocks for every technique, including fakes.

Indirect attack. The fighter incorporates the use of a "fake" to set up the kick. By faking a high attack (a), the opponent leaves the lower body unprotected (b), allowing the fighter to score.

Combination Attack

Attacking by combination involves more than simply stringing techniques together in groups of two, three, or more. To use this method, try putting together two modes of attack, such as a direct attack followed by a rhythm

Attack by combination. The fighter utilizes any two ways of attack. In this case, the fighter fakes a low kick (*a-b*) to set up an immobilization (*c-d*), rendering the opponent unable to attack.

disruption (see below), or an indirect attack followed by an attack by immobilization (see below). Begin your combination attack by doubling up on the jab or front-leg round kick. A jab-cross-hook combination is an all-time favorite attack by combination. Next, try a direct or indirect attack as a set-up followed by an immobilization attack.

Immobilization Attack

At some point during the first karate tournaments held during the early 1960s, the method of attack by immobilization became popular. Although it was not then known by its current name, the method was the same. Competitors would grab their opponents' gis and hold them in place (immobilization), then use a reverse punch or chop to score. Holding and hitting is the perfect way to neutralize an opponent's offense, improve accuracy, and increase dominant control by throwing a barrage of punches to his unprotected head and upper body.

Immobilization can also be attained when a kick or punch is used to strike an opponent in such a way as to render their kick or punch useless. Punch a fighter in the biceps, and you have temporarily immobilized their arm. Use a side kick to your opponent's hip or a shin kick to the upper thigh, and you might immobilize their leg.

Karate fighters have limited access to more sophisticated methods of immobilizing or trapping arms or legs. Often it's a good idea to supplement your karate style by adapting trapping skills from other systems such as escrima, wing chun, and jeet kune do.

Rhythm Disruption Attack

To use a rhythm disruption attack method, first develop a method to change the speed or timing (or both) of your technique during its delivery. A back fist that starts slow, then speeds up just before contact is an example of a change in speed.

A rhythm disruption attack technique disrupts the natural rhythm of your opponent. They might react to a slow strike but are unprepared to quickly adjust to a change in speed. You might also try executing a front kick that is converted into a round kick before contact is made. By changing direction during the execution of a technique, you create a rhythm disruption attack.

Using superior footwork often results in rhythm disruption as well. Try circling to your right several times, developing a highly anticipated pattern. As your opponent relaxes his guard in anticipation of your next move, change directions, breaking the flow of the match and allowing you to score.

Attack by immobilization. The fighter (*a*) immobilizes the opponent's arm (*b*), then strikes with a reverse punch (*c*) and a foot sweep (*d*). This combination was often used by tournament fighters in the 1960s and 1970s.

Rhythm disruption. The fighter attempts to lure the opponent into second-guessing the fighter's intentions. In this sequence, the fighter throws a predictable jab (*a*), repositions (*b*), and in setting up a rhythm throws the jab again (*c*). As the opponent relaxes after a second ineffective attack (*d*), the fighter quickly changes direction (*e*) and timing so that the opponent is unable to answer the attack in time (*f*).

KARATE AND MIXED MARTIAL ARTS COMPETITIONS

Since 1993, the concept of mixed martial arts tournaments has become popular in the United States. In most karate systems, long range—or what is more appropriately called "kickboxing range"—is preferred. For karateka to effectively compete in these tournaments, they must adjust to being out of their comfort zones. Mixed martial arts competitors must understand range. Karateka who enter mixed martial arts competitions must supplement skills at long range with skills in close trapboxing range and ground grappling.

Fighting range represents a conceptual measurement determined by the distance separating two combatants. Traditionally, martial arts instructors have maintained four designated ranges: kicking, punching, trapping, and grappling ranges. Through these four distinct classifications, the concept of range can be easily understood. However, the four measurements can be reduced to three categories to designate (1) combat from a distance, (2) in a standup clinch position, and (3) on the ground.

Long range or kicking range is the distance at which a fighter can kick but remain far enough away that typical boxing skills are virtually useless. At punching range, combatants can score easily with punches and close-range kicks. When opponents stand toe-to-toe, typical boxing skills often are dropped in favor of trapping or immobilization skills, including head butts and elbow and knee strikes. Often, if fighters cannot resolve the fight in this standup clinch, then the fight goes to the ground. Once this occurs, the term grappling range is used.

It's interesting to note that entire arts have been designed around specific ranges. Taekwondo and karate are most notably seen as long-range arts. Karate practitioners feel at ease at long range. Boxers, on the other hand, find little to do at long range and have little or no understanding of grappling range. Boxers are punching-range specialists. Finally, the arts of judo, wrestling, and Brazilian jiujitsu are functionally designed for grappling encounters.

Competing within range would be simple if karateka fought only karateka, grapplers fought only grapplers, and punchers fought only within medium range, but this is seldom the case. When matched in open competitions such as those seen in reality fights or in actual self-defense, the concept of range becomes difficult to define.

Experience shows that in open fighting or self-defense, there are really only three discernible ranges. Mixed martial arts competitions have demonstrated that three range designations can be more accurately described as kickboxing, trapboxing, and ground submissions (or grappling).

Kickboxing refers to a standup range in which kicking or punching is used. This is the range used in most forms of karate competition. Ground submissions are any altercation that takes place when two combatants are on the ground or mat. Ground submissions may include locks, holds, or chokes—classic grappling maneuvers. Ground submissions also include holding and hitting from a mount or guard position in what may be called a nonclassical grappling procedure or submissions boxing.

Trapboxing range is a new designation that combines boxing and trapping skills used in a standup clinch position. This range can be adapted to karate systems. When combat takes place in the reality fighting arena, a

Fighting from the clinch. The fighter (*a*) may choose to immobilize (*b*) or trap (*c*) the opponent's offensive weapons. By gaining control of the head (*d*), multiple unprotected strikes (*e*) such as the knee strike (*f*) can be employed to defeat the opponent.

new phenomenon occurs. Fighters go to the clinch and begin to hold and hit until they go to the ground or one fighter submits. This standup clinch position may lack the glamour of both trapping and boxing arts, but in actual self-defense efficiency is anything that scores. The standup clinch position needs to be developed by those who seek success in a physical encounter. To better understand this new fighting range, we need to reexamine the arts of boxing and trapping.

Bare Knuckle Boxing as a Martial Art

With the introduction of what is sometimes called either mixed martial arts or reality fighting—a bare knuckle event in which fighters employ various arts—the art of boxing again has become the subject of reexamination, and with good reason.

Bare knuckle fighting can be traced back several thousands of years before the birth of Christ. Some historians believe that the Greek term for making a box with the hands *(pyxis)*, a clenched fist, is the basis for the modern word boxing. Another source contends that a 13th-century Catholic priest, St. Bernadine, taught fist-fighting as an alternative to dueling and used the term "boxing up" in reference to the skill of blocking the opponent's punches or offense.

The first recorded bare knuckle fight in the United States took place in New York in 1816 (Hyer versus Beasly). Though illegal and unpopular, bare knuckle fighting gained some notoriety in the late 1880s, when the great John L. Sullivan traveled the country challenging all comers for a purse of several hundred dollars. Rules incorporating three-minute rounds, padded gloves, and no wrestling or gouging were sponsored by the Marquis of Queensbury in England in 1865. Eventually, these rules were accepted, and bare knuckle fighting found no mass support for more than 100 years.

In actual combat fighting, the boxer has several tools proven to be effective. Of course, the primary skills of the jab, hook, upper-cut, and cross are essential. However, the boxer's ability to fight from the clinch—in which two fighters are fully entangled in an upright position—is just now receiving adequate attention. The reason is simple. During reality fighting events, the combatants almost invariably go to the clinch. Fighters with skill in the clinch stay upright. Others go to the ground or mat.

In the clinch position, often called inside fighting or trench fighting, where fighters hold and hit (often out of exhaustion or desperation), skilled boxers understand that they can conserve energy, avoid taking any hard blows, and maneuver for better target access. Whenever boxers get in trouble, they're told to go to the clinch position. Often when a fighter is outmatched and cannot strike an opponent at boxing range, he or she goes immediately to the clinch to avoid absorbing any unnecessary punishment and to survive the fight. While sport boxers have long been successful in winning in the clinch, karateka often have neglected to recognize the importance of the trapboxing range and how arts can be combined for success.

The Art of Trapboxing

While the boxer has mastered the clinch to some degree, the trapping expert provides the missing components lacking in the boxer's arsenal. In boxing, the fighter is penalized for a head butt, holding and hitting, and so on. This is not true in the art of trapping.

Trapboxing. From the on-guard position (*a*), the fighter immobilizes the jab (*b*), then positions to tie up both of the opponent's hands (*c*). Ultimately the fighter gains the position to repeatedly strike an opponent (*d*) whose defense is completely immobilized.

The strategy for trapping is to temporarily immobilize the opponent's weapons and to follow that action with a direct hit. Trapping often involves slapping, holding, or redirecting the opponent's weapons in an attempt to gain distance, time, and position.

Remember that trapping, or immobilization, is one of the five ways of attack. Trapping bridges the gap and is not an end in itself. Although trapping is well suited for all karate styles, instructors may supplement the range by researching methods from other systems.

The weapons and tactics of the trapper include fists, fingers, forearms, feet, knees, elbows, kicks, head butts, biting, grabbing, pinching, takedowns, chokes, locks, and holds. The trapping expert takes the art of dirty fighting to an extreme, yet the trapper often lacks the components of mobility and defensive head positioning commonly used in boxing.

Because boxers are involved in the spontaneity of constant motion, they must learn the strategy of controlling an opponent's set point. The boxer also learns to fire weapons at odd angles and to control an opponent in the clinch. By combining the skills of trapping with those of boxing, one actualizes the commonality of both arts.

Unlike the classic trapper, the trapboxer often employs full-body immobilization, permitting the fighter to neutralize any offense put forth by his opponent. By holding an opponent in an unprotected position, the trapboxer can throw multiple strikes to achieve a knockout or submission. By locking, trapping, or immobilizing an opponent's neck or arm, the trapboxer can easily reposition to deny access to his

own targets while engaging full power to the opponent's vulnerable areas.

The trapboxer's primary strategy then is to neutralize the opponent's offense through immobilization (trapping) and positioning and mobility (boxing) and to deliver offensive strikes from the arsenals of both boxing and trapping. Mobility and increased firepower are the advantages to trapboxing. In the art of in-fighting, don't bet against the trapboxer.

In actual self-defense, as in mixed martial arts competition, there's no discernible difference between boxing and trapping ranges. The term "trapboxing" can refer to any standup fighting method that takes place in close. In view of the fact that most actual fights take place in close, it is wise for the prudent karateka to recognize the importance of trapboxing range and develop skills to become efficient in the art.

As the fighter blocks the jab (*a*), he evades or slips the opponent's right cross (*b*) and sets up a sweeping technique (*c-d*).

THE BEASLEY MATRIX FOR MARTIAL ARTS

When the karateka develops an understanding of the five ways of attack and the designations of fighting range, it becomes evident that most traditional systems are limited in application. For example, if your karate system has no structured method of trapping, you may find it difficult to properly execute attack by immobilization. Most karateka have been unsuccessful at mixed martial arts competitions primarily because they lack skills at the trapping range and ground submission range.

In the 1980s, I began writing articles about a concept I called the "martial arts matrix." The matrix is a system for cognitively discerning the utility of an art when placed in a grid plotting the needs of a situation and how the art could be adapted (see table 9.1). On the matrix, the art is listed on the far left. To the right of the listed art are the categories kickboxing, trapboxing, and ground submissions. Under each designation, list the skills within your system that are useful. Most karateka immediately find that their arts are range specific—that is, the focus of their art is intended for use in only one range.

To adapt any karate system to a matrix approach with skills that are competitive in sport or self-defense, you need to supplement the style with skills from other arts. A running theme of this book has been that modern karate must be independent of the limitations imposed by style. As independent karateka, we must let needs dictate the skills we choose. In the next chapter, we'll look at training methods used to advance the development of modern karate.

TABLE 9.1   The Beasley Matrix for Martial Arts Evaluation

The matrix is a system for cognitively discovering the utility of an art or technique when placed in a grid detailing certain factors and assigning values to each component.

Specific techniques or complete arts are listed to the left of the grid. The factors of range are listed to the right. Range can be scored as follows: 1 = primary use for the range; 2 = secondary use for the range; or 3 = not designed for this range. (Note that these scores are given for combat efficiency under street conditions.)

Two additional categories, personal preference (whether or not you prefer to use the skill) and WOO (window of opportunity), are listed to the right of range. Personal preference are scored as follows: 1 = high preference; 2 = acceptable; or 3 = low preference. When scoring the WOO factor, note that 1 = opportunity to the use the skill is high; 2 = occasional; and 3 = seldom. For example, you might score the jump spinning ax kick as "1," of high preference for your personal choice. However, for the WOO factor, the kick could score a "3," which means it can seldom be used. This represents little problem if you practice karate only for fitness and art. However, if you practice karate for sport or self defense, you may choose to consider deleting this technique as a serious tool for self defense.

(continued)

TABLE 9.1 *(continued)*

It should also be noted that, at times, environmental factors can influence the WOO factor. In a cold climate when the aggressor is heavily dressed in a hooded parka, the boxer's jab (which typically scores high in WOO) would do very little damage because of the padding from the hooded coat. In a crowded room, a stepping side kick would be almost impossible to perform even though you might score it as high in personal preference and high in WOO.

As you score each art or technique, go with your first impression. Do not ponder each score; just write it down. Remember, your score can change year by year as you gain more understanding of your personal attributes. Add all of the scores across the grid and divide the total score by 5.

The matrix is designed to help you more clearly develop a personal strategy. Think of the results as though you are getting back the scores of an eye exam. In an eye exam, the low score is great news. The arts or techniques that receive the lowest scores are the tools you will be able to use most effectively.

Taking all factors into account, I have plotted the following arts and techniques in two grids provided below. The founder of every style has a mental matrix, or grid, upon which he/she could plot each technique in a system. If your matrix does not match the founder's matrix, then you would be well advised to seek out another sensei or supplement any deficiencies by incorporating skills from other arts. It would be useful for all sensei to make their personal matrices available to students.

Matrix 1: Arts

Art	Kick-boxing range	Trap-boxing range	Ground range	Personal preference	Window of opportunity	Total
Karate	1	2	3	1	2	1.8
Hapkido	2	2	3	2	3	2.4
Judo (jiujitsu)	3	2	1	2	2	2
Boxing	3	1	3	1	1	1.8
Taekwondo	1	3	3	3	2	2.4
Kung fu	1	2	3	3	3	2.4
Aikido	3	2	3	3	3	2.8

For me, the lowest scores were given for karate (1.8), boxing (1.8), and judo (2). My system of karate combines these three arts. You may have a different score and still have a very complete art.

TABLE 9.1 *(continued)*

Matrix 2: Techniques

Technique	Kick-boxing range	Trap-boxing range	Ground range	Personal preference	Window of oppor-tunity	Total
Jab	1	1	3	1	1	1.4
Cross	1	2	1	1	1	1.2
Hook	1	1	1	1	1	1
Front kick	1	2	3	1	1	1.6
Round kick	1	3	3	1	1	1.6
Side kick	1	2	3	1	2	1.8
Jump spin hook kick	2	3	3	3	3	2.8
Jump spin ax kick	2	3	3	3	3	2.8
Low block	1	2	3	3	3	2.4
High block	3	3	3	3	3	3
Sparring (contact)	1	1	1	1	1	1
Sparring (one-step)	1	1	1	2	1	1.2
Kata	3	3	3	3	3	3
Focus pad	1	1	2	1	1	1.2

Here are some common karate techniques and training methods. Note that I have a preference for the hook (1) and the cross, or reverse punch (1.2). I have little faith in the jump spin kicks (2.8), the high block (3), and the practice of kata (3) for improving combat efficiency. (Each receives a high WOO score, suggesting that they have limited use.) I have scored sparring and focus pad training as my preferred training methods. Your scores might be different from mine, and that is perfectly all right. Karate performance and preference always will reflect individual choices. Only when your ability to reach your peak performance is limited by the style do you experience problems.

Training Methods of Modern Karate

During its formative years, karate training in the United States closely followed the training methods passed down generation to generation from 19th-century martial artists. These methods required monotonous repetitions of basic skills, and the karate student was often asked to train outside or on hardwood floors. The more undesirable the conditions, it was thought, the better the opportunity to weed out all but the most dedicated students.

Moreover, students were expected to rely only on self-styled training aids for special improvement. The *makiwara*, a length of rope tied around a tree or post, was employed in place of a heavy bag. The practitioner was required to strike the makiwara daily to develop callused fists and feet. Studies have shown that such practices result in serious bone damage and other ailments. Instructors of the time emphasized rejecting anything modern or, more specifically, anything that the ancient masters did not use themselves.

The use of weights was also considered taboo, as flexibility is essential in karate, and they believed that weights tightened the muscles. While athletes in other sports were reaping the benefits of controlled modern training aids and weight training, most karate practitioners refused to add modern methods to their supplemental routines.

Granted, the old school methods produced some outstanding performers—but they also discouraged many American students. The training methods initially inhibited the development of karate in the United States because they did not allow athletic Americans to reach their full potential.

Contemporary training methods are designed to produce specific results. Studies show that self-defense, sport, and physical fitness are the three primary objectives for Americans who choose karate training. As a result, training methods are designed accordingly. Training sessions should last approximately an hour and be done at least twice a week, preferably more. For best results, each session should be intense, with little or no wasted time.

Simply stated, the concept of specificity of training is based on the proven idea that one achieves success in those areas most often practiced. In other words, you're best able to perform specifically the tasks you have trained to perform. Weightlifting, jogging, sprinting, and calisthenics may well prove to be beneficial for conditioning martial artists, but they won't necessarily improve their ability to defend themselves. To become proficient in self-defense, you need to specifically train the areas most associated with the spontaneity of self-defense. Contact sparring more clearly resembles the spontaneous and unrehearsed quality of self-defense than other methods of karate training.

SPARRING

Methods of free sparring may vary. While one school might prefer tournament play—for example, point karate—others choose contact karate or kickboxing competition. Thus, while individual skills are constantly used (for example, a round kick is often employed in a form, in point sparring, and in full-contact practice), the exact interpretation varies according to the intent of the individual performer.

Whereas in kata the practitioner moves against an imaginary opponent, sparring requires the ability to react to an opponent. The ability to react and choose the appropriate skill or combination of skills is essential to becoming a true master.

Sparring can take several forms. Technique sparring allows partners to practice skills on one another in a controlled environment. Self-defense sparring and combat sparring provide opportunities to react to opponents.

Sparring as a method of training for karate enthusiasts is a relatively modern phenomenon. There are several common methods of sparring: prearranged self-defense sparring, classic noncontact sparring, point sparring, and full-contact sparring. The strategies for competition discussed in chapter 9 are useful for advancing in all forms of sparring.

Prearranged Self-Defense Sparring

In prearranged self-defense sparring, one participant assumes an attacking position—a punch, kick, or holding maneuver—while a defender attempts to block and counter or escape. Most beginners are instructed in prearranged sparring drills. Prearranged sparring lacks spontaneity and is highly structured in its approach. However, it can be valuable as a first step in learning self-defense or in performing a specific counter should it ever be necessary to actually perform it.

There's also a hidden value to prearranged self-defense sparring. Karateka who can assume a state of mind that makes the scenario seem real, if only for a few seconds, participate in training the mind to become empty, thus actualizing the highest level of karate. Unfortunately, most students simply go through the drills at the physical level, never attempting to train the mind.

More recently, self-defense experts have incorporated new drills, including verbal assaults and physical encounters with fully padded attackers, and have greatly improved the usefulness of self-defense sparring. These experts believe that the participation in what has been called "adrenal stress training" (chapter 8) trains the mind more effectively, as the scenario resembles a real-life situation. In actuality, the theme remains the same: causing a feeling of distress. While in a state of distress, the participant must conquer negative emotions, such as immobilization, helplessness, fear, anxiety, and anger, replacing them with feelings of peace, control, power, and emptiness (the unobstructed mind). No doubt, a greater number of participants can come to experience lower levels of distress in a shorter period of time by incorporating the modern training methods for self-defense.

It's possible that the emotion produced during adrenal stress training is short lived and must be revalidated at different intervals. No research is currently available on this subject. The formality and security of the karate dojo provides an environment in which emotional control is developed over an extended period of time. Perhaps the best advice is to participate in both forms of training.

Classic Noncontact Sparring

In noncontact sparring, opponents are free to move about in an unrehearsed manner. Punches and kicks are thrown at predetermined target areas (usually the front of the head and body) and are pulled or stopped before actual contact is made. Noncontact sparring requires no contact or safety gear. The method lacks the element of reality in that, when no contact is made, participants are not conditioned to strike a target or to withstand the effect of a karate blow.

Noncontact sparring is appropriate for all levels as a warm-up method. In the early 1960s, noncontact rules often resulted in hard contact and what was called "blood and guts" matches as referees exercised tremendous diversity in how they scored points.

Point Sparring With Contact

Perhaps the most popular method of sparring practice is point karate. In point sparring, participants wearing protective gear on their hands and feet make light contact to predetermined target areas. Each time a target is struck by a blow, the match is stopped, and the person striking the opponent's target is awarded a point.

Point sparring with contact. In dojo or in open competition, fighters develop mobility and accuracy in performing skills. Use of safety equipment ensures that injuries will be minimal. Here, world champion Steve "Nasty" Anderson, who dominated 1980s point competitions, easily slips out of the way of Jim Butin.

Both noncontact sparring and point sparring allow students to develop mobility and accuracy in performing karate skills. The concept of light-contact point karate originated from noncontact karate practice in 1973, when sport karate promoter Mike Anderson required the use of safety equipment for all black-belt competitors.

As tournament fighters became accustomed to the safety gear in the 1970s and 1980s, many of the training methods were redesigned to better equip the performer with sparring skills. As practitioners found they could effectively withstand karate blows cushioned by the safety gear, they devised the concept of full-contact karate.

Full-Contact Sparring

Full-contact karate differs from other methods of sparring in that blows are not pulled and contestants are not stopped after each exchange. With modern training aids, full-contact karate can be practiced quite safely. As contact is made during practice, the student reacts to the contact when hit and learns to deliver efficient blows as he or she hits an opponent. Contact sparring allows a more realistic method of testing and evaluating the level of proficiency a student has achieved.

In 1974, the Professional Karate Association (PKA) sanctioned the first world full-contact karate competitions. The sport of full-contact karate lasted from 1973 through the mid-1980s. The PKA rules favored karate kicks above the waist (no leg kicks). Many fighters lost rounds because of a failure-to-kick rule. Full-contact karate gave way to kickboxing as fighters became

The Professional Karate Association introduced full-contact karate in 1974. These fighters are engaged in a non-title full-contact match.

National champion Jay Bell (left) demonstrates that, in competition, techniques must be altered to best meet the circumstances.

better trained in boxing skills and leg kicks, which were forbidden in PKA full-contact karate rules. Today the term "kickboxing" refers to all forms of full-contact, stand-up fighting. To differentiate kickboxing from PKA full-contact karate, simply recognize that all competitions before the mid-1980s in which leg kicks were forbidden were full-contact karate. Competitions in which leg kicks were permitted were classified as kickboxing. The possible exception to this rule would be the Oyama-influenced styles that have traditionally incorporated leg kicks. Since 1993 (primarily due to the popularity of mixed martial arts competitions), leg kicks to the thigh increasingly have become a part of most karate methods.

Just short of actual street encounters, full-contact sparring represents hands-on experience. In contact sparring, individual style can be encouraged. While quality contact sparring is essential to modern karate, it's often neglected or reduced to the performance of training drills. The following factors may aid in developing functional contact training.

Sparring Partner

Select a good partner or partners. Some partners are valued because they're not aggressive and allow you to work on your offensive game. Other partners might be selected because they are always coming at you and inviting counterattacks. In some cases, sparring partners may be chosen because they lack strength or skill and afford you the opportunity to practice defense (slipping, weaving, etc.). At other times, a stronger or more experienced fighter allows you to test your skills.

Regardless of your choice, partners should be spontaneous and not simply perform drills that often are used for focus pads. Try to achieve the state of mushin. Be relaxed in your thoughts, but fight hard. Plan a strategy, use the ways of attack, and be creative. Try new methods and techniques. Get a partner you like, and spend time together fighting.

Protective Equipment

If you spar, you're going to get hit. Expect to get hit, but don't expect to get hurt. Practice training drills before you begin sparring so that you develop a good defense. Once you begin to spar, attempt to make good contact.

Invest in high-quality protective equipment, such as a professional head protector. Some head protectors come with chin bars to give more protection. Head gear with full plastic face guards are for drills, not for actual sparring. In actual sparring, the plastic fogs up. Some people wear motorcycle helmets during drills. A motorcycle helmet might be dangerous in spontaneous contact sparring because the weight of the helmet causes extra stress to the neck.

Boxers have more experience in contact sparring, so stick with quality boxing equipment (head gear, mouth piece, etc.). Gloves should be 16 to 20 ounces. Larger gloves give more protection. Most boxers also wear shin and ankle protection. You can add forearm and elbow pads, depending on which body parts you'll use as weapons. If you intend to perform hard contact, use professional, tested equipment.

Distance

Generally speaking, you can best work on kicking skills at longer range and boxing skills at shorter range. You'll quickly find that the most functional range is toe to toe. This range is called "in-fighting" or "trapboxing" (see previous chapter). At long range, you can get hit hard with the jab, cross, and all kicks. At close range, hooks, knees, and elbows work best. In close, you can work on head positions and the trapboxing methods of holding and hitting.

In-fighting is a sophisticated art. An experienced full-contact fighter will often want to experience an opponent up close. In-fighting is safe and challenging for the experienced fighter, but beginners should avoid in-fighting except with equally matched partners. While most beginners start at kicking range, a better way to begin is toe to toe. Learn the in-fighting skills first. You might get hit more often at first, but you'll seldom get hit as hard as you will at long range. Since combat often begins face to face, the person with in-fighting experience has an advantage.

Advanced karate practitioners interested in self-defense should train in full-contact sparring. Full-contact sparring is also essential to success in mixed martial arts competitions. As karateka attain skill in full-contact sparring, they often develop a sense of individuality contrary to the group attitude necessary for the traditional practice of karate. In a school with a highly regimented social system in which rewards for advanced rank do not rely solely on physical skill, the social status system can and should be maintained. Our goal in karate should never be simply to develop a skilled fighter. We want to always strive to develop disciplined character as well.

KATA TRAINING

The practice of modern forms and patterns, in which students mimic a battle against multiple antagonists, may vary considerably from school to school. Kata has become the single most controversial facet of karate practice. Traditionalists claim that kata is the basis of all karate—and they are right. In the kata can be found all the skills for the style. Kata is an excellent method for training large groups in coordinated fashion so that all students learn the proper execution of acceptable skills employed in the style.

Kata provides a good measure for advancement from one grade to the next. Some people have claimed that kata are used to hide secret techniques so that members from opposing schools won't recognize the true meaning of a strike. One theory suggests that the Okinawans refused to teach the full interpretation of the kata to those outside Okinawan styles. As a result, karate kata introduced in the United States included several blocking and striking techniques that, to an experienced fighter, more resembled a dance than a fight.

The problem of interpreting kata is compounded by the fact that many books and videotapes demonstrate kata blocks and strikes that simply would not work in any but the most controlled situations. The idea presented in basic kata is that a person attacks you from the left side and, to retaliate, you perform a low block and follow up with a step-through punch. To perform these awkward moves during real combat seems unrealistic. It's no wonder that so many modern stylists have abandoned the traditional kata.

In the 1980s, artists including Seiyu Oyata from Okinawa and long-time American kata master George Dillman (formerly a student of Oyata), introduced the concept of no blocks in the kata. According to this new interpretation, kata contained no blocks—what for years had been thought to be a block was actually a grappling technique used to set up a pressure-point attack. Dillman and many of his followers presented unique and innovative interpretations of kata, attracting much-deserved attention.

At all levels of performance, kata exists as a method of dramatization. You must imagine an attack. As long as the response (*bunkai* or interpretation) makes sense to the performer, much can be gained through practicing kata.

In the 1970s, tournament competitors innovated an interpretation of kata as musical forms. In musical forms, the performer creates a series

1980s world kata champion John Chung performs a world-class kata. In performing the kata, one must visualize an opponent.

of attacks and defenses choreographed to pulsating musical themes. Musical forms as a method of training represents an excellent way to improve aerobic conditioning while maintaining both performer and spectator interest.

For any program of exercise, sport, or self-defense to be successful, it must have a sense of purpose. Practitioners must know that what they're doing has results that are valuable to them. The traditional kata represented a pie in the sky mentality. Practitioners did not always know why they performed the skills; rather, they believed that if they persevered, the kata would lead them to a higher level of understanding. Thus, kata became the source of many arguments. Many people felt that after they had invested years improving their ability to block and strike through the kata method, the method was worth defending. Others simply abandoned the practice. Both the Dillman method and the concept of musical forms have given a new sense of purpose to the interpretations of kata.

FOCUS PAD TRAINING

By incorporating drills that include the use of a focus pad, bag, or other object, karateka can readily observe a measurable result in training. Being able to see an immediate result provides a sense of purpose. Focus pads work at both the anaerobic and aerobic levels. Moreover, drills can be designed to simulate actual conditions for kickboxing, trapboxing, ground submissions, and self-defense. Advanced focus pad drills with as many as fifteen

Focus pad training. Drills are used to simulate actual sparring conditions. Here, Joe Lewis trains with the author.

or more strikes have replaced kata for many practitioners of the nonclassical school of karate.

To introduce focus pad drills, the instructor asks the class to form two lines. The line facing the instructor is line A. The line facing away from the instructor is line B. The students in line A hold focus mats. At the instructor's signal, students in both lines assume a ready position. The instructor then calls out, "Fighting position!" The students in line A hold the focus pads, while the students in line B strike the pads. After 8 to 10 repetitions, both lines return to ready position. The focus pads are given to the students in line B. The drills continue until all techniques are completed.

Using focus pads produces measurable improvements over the commonly used practice of kicking and punching the air or an imaginary opponent. Drills can be arranged to reflect free sparring by coaching one student to hold the pads while another student moves around, striking targets in a spontaneous manner as they are presented. Focus pad drills can be designed similar to free-form kata in which both the performer and the coach (who holds the pad) move about in a prearranged manner.

THE HEAVY BAG

World karate champion Bill Wallace works out on the traditional heavy bag.

If a training partner is not available, the karateka may choose to strike a heavy bag. When striking the bag, be sure to wear protective gloves. Move around the bag, snapping a kick or a punch out and back, then quickly reposition to simulate actual sparring. I often tell students that the strategy for striking a bag or pad (or another fighter) is not unlike striking a hornets' nest. You would not walk up to a hornets' nest, strike the nest with a stick, then stand in the same position to count how many hornets died. The remaining hornets would quickly identify you as a target. If you strike another person, he or she is most likely to strike you back if you remain in the same position. Move! Strike, snap your kick or punch, and reposition. Use this concept when striking a focus pad or bag and when sparring.

TRAINING PRINCIPLES FOR MODERN KARATE

The American Independent Karate Instructors Association (AIKIA) has identified 12 principles that reflect modern independent training procedures. The word "independent" is used to suggest that the school is free of a fixed method or style. To use the modern American karate terminology, they "use what works." The 12 principles follow.

1. Observance of traditional practices. Independent practitioners maintain a base style (Japanese, Korean, Okinawan, Chinese, etc.). They practice the concept of kata and other appropriate training methods to maintain a karate format.

2. Chain of command. To facilitate a character-enhancement program, independent practitioners observe belt rank and acquired status in the dojo.

3. Mobile fighting position. Independent stylists use a modern boxing/kickboxing stance. All techniques are practiced in the fighting position.

4. Constantly shifting footwork. Mobility is essential to realistic self-defense or competition. Footwork drills are practiced and maintained constantly. The independent stylist glides across the floor in constant motion.

World champion Kathy Long demonstrates the round kick.

5. Nontelegraphic/nonchambering principles. Contrary to most traditional skills, the majority of independent techniques emphasize the elusive and deceptive qualities of being nontelegraphic. Techniques are not chambered (brought back to the hip or held in a telegraphic manner).

6. Weapons-first principle. Emphasis is placed on moving the weapon (back fist, jab, kick, etc.) first, without chambering. In traditional kata, the body moves first, followed by the weapon only after a secure stance is attained. Independent stylists initiate the weapon first, making it difficult for the opponent to identify the skill.

147

7. Principles of attack. Rather than simply execute a technique, the modern fighter constantly assesses the opponent's position and approaches or closes the gap by using the five ways of attack: direct, indirect, combination, immobilization, and rhythm disruption.

8. Concept of range. Independent stylists train at all three fighting ranges: kickboxing (long range); trapboxing (close range); and ground submissions.

9. Integration of multicultural arts and boxing. For the modern karateka, knowledge comes from many sources, regardless of the country of origin. The independent stylist may perform knee techniques from Thai boxing, punching skills from western boxing, and ground submissions from Brazilian jiujitsu. He or she takes the tool, gives credit to the source, and then brings it into his or her own system, changing the delivery as necessary.

10. Use of technological advances. Modern karateka use technological advances, including focus pads, upright striking apparatus, standing and hanging bags, and so on. Intricate drills are developed to express the participant's needs in combat. Karateka can supplement their instruction through the use of videotapes, compact discs, progressive resistance machines, technologically advanced gear (weapons, etc.), nutritional supplements, cross training, and other progressive methods that enhance training.

11. Use of safety equipment. While old-school karateka may have practiced barefoot in open air dojos, modern karateka use safety protection, including boxing gloves, head gear, shin protection, and the like.

12. Emphasis on contact sparring. By using safety gear, the modern independent karateka can engage in full-contact sparring. Sparring allows the karateka to develop an individual understanding and application of attributes and strategies.

Karate training methods have greatly advanced during the fifty years in which the art has been practiced in the United States. The American Independent Karate Instructors Association (AIKIA), established in 1979, has become the leading advocate for independent thinking and the promotion of progressive concepts for karate training. All of the principles in this book support and reflect the AIKIA philosophy of training and teaching the art and sport of both classical and nonclassical karate.

Teaching

In the traditional karate dojo, the sensei maintains total authority. While his or her main task is to teach students karate, sometimes the roles of counselor, confidante, first-aid provider, caregiver, and spiritual advisor are assumed. A sensei must also be a salesman, motivational speaker, and accountant, overseeing matters such as advertising and public relations. Sometimes he or she is also a custodian and maintenance man.

Some instructors of karate have entered the teaching profession on a part-time basis. Others have made teaching their lifetime career. Rarely, if ever, will you find the position of sensei advertised in the classified ads of a newspaper. For the most part, it takes an entrepreneur to become a sensei.

Most sensei have low to moderate incomes. Very few become wealthy. However, there is status and power involved in being the sensei. For most, the real payback is pride and enjoyment in the success, confidence, discipline, and maturity of their students. Many students' lives have been significantly enhanced because they were fortunate enough to be students of a dedicated sensei.

The majority of traditional karate instructors (perhaps as high as 80 percent) are male. Increasingly, women are becoming successful as sensei in modern karate dojos. A more recent trend is that, while women continue to be active students and black belts in the traditional dojo, when given the opportunity to teach they often opt to become instructors of aerobic kickboxing and other cardio-karate style fitness programs. Many black belts who are women choose to teach children's classes or women-only, adult self-defense programs. However, women can be equally as effective as men in teaching traditional karate.

STUDENT MOTIVATION

It's important for instructors to understand what motivates their students. Studies show many motivating factors for taking karate instruction. To learn self-defense is by far the most common. Most people have a degree of anxiety about the unknown. They wonder what they would do if they were attacked. Karate addresses self-defense on two levels. First, karate skills *are* effective in self-defense encounters. Second, and perhaps more important, those who take karate for years become much more aware of potential sources of danger and can thus avoid them. For instance, they are less likely to engage in aggressive behavior than someone who has not been trained in karate.

Competing is another reason students want to learn karate. All students of karate compete on a personal level, challenging themselves to improve their skills. Typically, our greatest opponent is the ego; many people realize they can improve themselves in several ways by learning to overcome the ego. Of course some students of karate, though perhaps as few as 25 percent, also compete in formal tournaments.

Many Americans are fitness conscious. Former karate champion and movie star Billy Blanks affected the lives of millions who purchased his *Tae Bo* martial arts/fitness/dance videos. Health clubs compete against the karate dojo for the fitness/martial arts market. Karate has much to offer Americans who want to improve their fitness levels.

Some people enter the dojo to learn Asian culture. Most Asian instructors stress an understanding of Japanese, Korean, and Chinese cultures as part of the karate program. Perhaps a majority of karate sensei teach at least some Oriental cultural practices, such as the bow. Karate is identified with the East and recognizes its history is a mystery to many Westerners.

Some karate students want to express their individuality through karate. For children, being identified as a karateka can provide a sense of self-efficacy and help build self-esteem. Adults, too, enjoy the recognition that being a karate student brings. They express themselves in ways they have learned in the dojo.

Karate has long been identified as a way to improve the self. Many parents enroll their children after seeing a dojo ad stating that children in the art learn self-defense, discipline, and confidence, which often translate into improved grades at school.

Some people sign up for karate lessons to seek revenge against another—the school bully, an attacker, a rival, or an unknown aggressor. Most karate movie producers incorporate revenge into their themes. Revenge is strong motivation. Fortunately, as the student becomes empowered through karate, the need for revenge and retaliation subsides considerably.

Karate instruction is becoming increasingly useful for employees in the fields of fitness, security, law enforcement, and education. Recently, the airline industry has started to encourage employees to learn self-defense methods.

STUDENT LEARNING

People learn for different reasons and at different rates. They learn through different ways. Some students do better with personal attention, whereas others are most affected by group attitudes and peer pressure. Some rely heavily on role modeling and constructive reinforcement of values and beliefs. Athletic students might pick up quickly on skills. Quiet or shy students might be easiest to mold into the karate persona.

Some students learn best through planned activities. Karate students must become actively involved in the dojo. After-class socials, informal pre-class meetings, carpooling, group attendance at martial arts movies and tournaments, self-defense demonstrations, and fundraising events are all ways in which dojo members can bond outside class. The dojo promotes a family unity. The dojo is a place of security that encourages students to actively participate. As I sometimes put it, students who kick together in class stick together out of class. Activity builds motivation and a desire to belong in the group.

Instructors need to be careful of the topics of conversation permitted in the dojo. Students quickly learn what the sensei approves of and disapproves of, what he demands and what he forbids. Topics that build citizenship, love of country, positive involvement in sports, family, church, school, and the like are topics that tend to improve character. Racist behavior or remarks and other prejudiced or intolerant acts demonstrate a lack of character. The sensei seeks to be aware of the students' conversations, enforcing and supporting healthy attitudes and discouraging negative discussions.

Repetition is a key factor in learning skills. In the early years of karate instruction, the sensei employed monotonous repetition to weed out the less-motivated students. Even weak students can become strong if they are reinforced and motivated to continue. Repetition provides a sense of security for some students. They learn the drills and feel comfortable performing them. Key points for improvement are demonstrated, discussed, and performed repetitiously.

A change in environment can help some students retain information. Learning a single skill, such as the front kick, may grow boring if the class repeats it many times. Repetition in such a case can be discouraging for some. Change the environment. Practice the same kick in the air, against a focus pad, while moving up and down the floor, against a partner, in one step, or in sparring. Try lying down and performing the front kick. Bring in a different target (paper, rope, or stick) for a new way of repeating an old skill. Whenever students seem to lose attention, change the environment.

Lecture

In the dojo, lecture is useful for building attitudes and discussing the history of a skill or style, but limit lectures to a few minutes at the beginning or end of class time. Class time is best spent on *doing*. All skills must be demonstrated and explained before students are expected to perform them. Typically, the sensei is skilled in the execution of each technique. Be aware that the way you demonstrate the skill is the way the students will perform it. Encourage students to demonstrate skills to provide examples that apply directly to specific ranks. One method that's encouraging is to take one or two students, depending on the exercise, and ask them to perform as the rest of the class watches. As the students perform, compliment them to encourage others to participate, provide explanations, and ask the class to applaud their efforts. Everyone smiles and enjoys the applause.

Dramatization

Dramatization involves acting out parts. Kata is dramatization, as the kata performer acts out a fight sequence. Moving up and down the floor while performing technique drills is dramatization. Kicking or punching the air is dramatization. Dramatization is useful for learning, but it limits understanding because the imaginary target provides no feelings, no sense of threat or danger, and no opportunity or need to adjust in order to compensate for an opponent or to otherwise react spontaneously. An Internet correspondent told me (though I suspect he made this up!) of a client who reported lifting 5-pound potato sacks in each hand 20 times each. The client reported that, within just a few days, he began to use 10-pound sacks, and by the end of the week he had advanced to using 50-pound sacks, one in each hand, lifting the sacks above his head 50 times each. The client reported that he was so pleased with his quick progress that the following week he was going to put potatoes in the sacks.

Like demonstration and explanation, dramatization is limited in its application for learning interpersonal skills to use when a situation changes or arises suddenly, such as an unexpected confrontation with a hostile aggressor.

Simulated Experience

In the dojo it's advisable to explain and demonstrate skills, and then allow students to try them out. Learning improves when a student simulates the experience against another person or against an object. One-step sparring, self-defense attacks, focus pad drills, and controlled sparring are forms of simulated experience. The more realistic the drill, the more effective the skill becomes for actual use.

Hands-on Experience

Hands-on experience is the highest form of learning. The sensei should provide opportunities to engage in hands-on activities during each class. Fighting against a partner enhances understanding of self-defense. (Do make sure both fighters are fully attired in protective gear.) Beginning students who participate in a no-threat sparring match with the sensei or an assistant, in which the sensei or assistant does not hit back, report they had no idea accuracy was so difficult to attain. Beginners often are exhausted after only a minute of no-threat sparring.

Advanced students should engage in contact sparring. Require ample protective gear, limit offensive weapons, and closely control the agreed-upon rules. Students become better at spontaneous encounters and emotional control through graduated steps in development.

Some students learn well by watching themselves on video. Tape their performances and show them the video, highlighting their strengths and weaknesses. All students need to practice away from the dojo. Equipment for practicing at home might include a heavy bag, weights, a stretching machine, a collection of martial arts books and magazines, and a library of martial arts instructional videos.

Seminars and Tournaments

Sensei should invite guest instructors highly skilled at a specific technique or fighting range to teach the class. Develop community co-ops that encourage instructors to share their specialty areas and supplement what they're teaching their classes. Also encourage students to attend seminars as a group. For a more advanced experience, groups might attend a martial arts summer camp. The sensei can teach, participate, or support class members during or after instruction at seminars. The concept of the road trip builds esprit de corps among students. A sensei who gives his best to support students won't feel threatened or intimidated by students learning from other talented individuals.

Tournaments can be productive learning experiences. It's best to select a few quality tournaments for participation rather than require constant competition. The tournament, like the seminar and summer camp, can be a costly investment for students, so they will need a sense of purpose.

Students learn in so many ways. In each case, the learning experience should nurture a sense of character and skill development. Using a variety of methods makes learning more interesting. Creating and maintaining a sense of purpose for each activity will give students the desire to continue.

THE EFFECTIVE SENSEI

Many of today's sensei differ from the sensei of the 1950s, 1960s, and 1970s. In the first few decades of development, the sensei was portrayed as a superhero, a role that could not be attained. The sensei was expected to be able to defeat all comers, know something about everything, and automatically enjoy the respect and loyalty of all students. According to movies and myth, he was a symbolic king, and in his kingdom called the dojo he exercised complete control. This role could not be lived up to. It's ridiculous. Today's sensei is an educator and a motivational role model. Many sensei are businessmen or businesswomen.

Like a coach, the sensei must instill discipline. Today's sensei knows he or she must earn respect. Like all teachers, the sensei exercises great influence on the students. Some sensei find it difficult to handle the attention and evoke claims of grandeur and delusions that they are much more than simply servant teachers. The ethical sensei must avoid personal relationships with students outside of the learning environment when the relationship involves monetary exchange, sexual involvement, or other situations in which the outcome highly favors the sensei, alters the student/teacher relationship, or results in the absence from or termination of class for the students.

The effective sensei is a skilled teacher and communicator who has developed superb knowledge in the field and can clearly convey this information to others. The sensei must exercise control of the classroom. "Martial" means military. Military discipline, when effectively applied, instills self-discipline and builds character. Discipline should first be verbal. Make eye contact with the student. Use body language that indicates seriousness (arms crossed, hands on hips, stern facial expression). Quickly and assertively tell the student to stop the inappropriate behavior. The behavior should cease.

Requiring a student or class to do pushups is a time-tested and common method of discipline. When I have had to discipline a college class, they tell me that they appreciate my concerns. I tell them, "I don't want to have to do this. It takes up your class time." I ask them, "Do you understand why you're

The effective sensei. Joe Lewis painstakingly guides the author through performance of the side kick.

doing pushups?" They shout, "Yes, sir! We failed, sir!" I ask, "Then what do you want to do?" They yell out, "Pushups, sir!" If they don't do the pushups correctly, they must begin again. When properly administered, doing pushups is a disciplinary exercise that builds unity. Often, students applaud after completing a disciplinary action. I explain to them that failure in the classroom transfers into failure in life. They usually agree and want to improve.

A "time-out" is another useful method of discipline. Once I had a young student whose mother thought nothing of bringing him to class late. While his mother watched from her car, I bowed the child in and then had him stand at the door in a time-out, unable to enter the drill in progress. The child understood. His mother stopped the car, opened the dojo door, and told the child to leave the class. He refused. I said nothing. She left and was never late again. All the children in the class learned a valuable lesson. When in the dojo, the instructor is in charge of carrying out the rules. Rules are obeyed. Discipline builds character and is essential to karate as a military art.

Repetition of skill performance is necessary but can become boring. The sensei must motivate through voice, body language, and active participation in all aspects of learning. The effective sensei motivates students to reach a higher level of performance. Yelling out instructions, speaking quietly, encouraging each student's individuality, and inspiring the whole group to express approval and unity are ways of increasing student motivation.

The effective sensei is a leader. Classes begin and end on time. Students are always aware of expectations—what is required of them in each drill for each rank. The sensei should be able to perform any skill or task that he asks

Under the supervision of sensei Joe Lewis, Jerry Beasley delivers the side kick in contest.

his students to perform. The class gives him respect, not because of his rank or position but because he has earned it as their leader.

The effective sensei must set a good example for students who desire to someday become sensei. The old saying, "Those who can do, and those who can't, teach," does not apply to the sensei. He or she should be able to do all that is taught. The attributes of bushido such as honesty, courage, veracity, and loyalty should be mirrored in his or her daily life.

The sensei should look the part and should strive to maintain physical fitness. He or she should dress the part, representing the art to the extent of his or her ability. Finally, a sensei should never allow his or her skill level to diminish. Teaching and learning are lifelong processes. It takes time, perseverance, and dedication to build character. Those who lack perseverance often prefer teaching short-term classes, seminars, or eclectic self-defense styles. To teach true karate, to assist students in attaining the empty mind, requires persistence and dedication to a single task.

BUILDING CHARACTER

Building character is a unique side effect of martial arts training. To build character in students, the sensei must ensure 10 conditions within the dojo.

1. Role modeling. Students require a sensei they can emulate, respect, and imitate.

It is important for the student to recognize a role model. Here, the author with one of the greatest karate role models of all time, Chuck Norris.

2. Goal setting and completing tasks. The rank system is designed to present a clear attainable set of goals. Each goal should include a demonstrated degree of difficulty. The basis of character is demonstrated as goals are met.

3. Recognition. A system of task completion and goal attainment is best supported through external recognition of success. The belt system provides external recognition.

4. Group interaction. Working together as a group unites students. Typically, students gather in cliques based on rank. Strong support groups, which may include friends and parents, spouses, and other family members, provide additional support and recognition for achievements in the dojo.

5. A degree of risk (a possibility of failure). When there's risk involved, achieving status becomes more meaningful. Distress associated with rank exams, tournament competition, or a high degree of difficulty in practice (kata in the snow, 100 kumite, etc.) can be effective for forging the spirit and loyalty of the group.

6. Self-discipline. This is an attribute to be valued. To build self-discipline, the sensei administers discipline consistently and without favoritism.

7. Class discussion. Discussion in class should focus on loyalty, respect, and other positive characteristics the sensei wants to promote. Negative comments, gossip, slander, and other such trash talk should not be permitted in the dojo.

8. Time in grade. This refers to the actual time in which a specific grade is held. Typically, kyu rank requires three to four months, while some dan ranks require five or more years in grade. To develop wisdom, there is no substitute for time spent in grade for the refinement of required behavior and skills.

9. Developing motivation. Motivational factors include respect, a sense of belonging, status, loyalty, success, and a sense of purpose. These attributes should be present among the students of the dojo.

10. Desire. Motivation, achievement, and desire go together. To advance to the next rank might seem easy for some. Achievement implies more than simple advancement. Achievement is the result of desire. Students who achieve rank through hard work develop respect for the art, the sensei, the dojo, and themselves. A belt system based primarily on perceived monetary gain and time in grade fails to build healthy desire.

STUDENT RANKS

A typical student ranking system includes 10 kyus or grades. The lowest rank is 10; 1 is the highest. The 10th kyu (or *gup* in Korean karate) is awarded a white belt; ranks 9, 8, and 7, a yellow, orange, or gold belt; ranks 6, 5, and 4, a green, blue, or purple belt; and the senior student ranks of 3, 2, and 1, a brown or red belt.

By practicing two to three times per week with the sensei, the beginning student usually progresses from one rank to the next every three to four months. A student could enter training for the first dan after 30 to 36 months of continued instruction. When a student drops out of the class, his or her rank is forfeited after about six months (because skills diminish with little or no practice). Since requirements at different schools can vary, a student who changes from one school to another typically must begin at the white-belt level again or work at the current rank until meeting the requirements to advance to the next level in the new style.

Classes

Classes begin with fitness, endurance, and flexibility drills (approximately 15 minutes) for warm-up. Students line up according to rank, with highest ranks at the front and right of the class and lowest ranks in the back. Most modern schools offer classes that are rank specific so that all beginners in ranks 10, 9, 8, and 7 practice together. A second class is offered for intermediate grades of 6, 5, and 4. A third class is offered for senior students in grades 3, 2, and 1. After the warm-up, which is typically the same for each class, instruction begins.

Most classes consist of review and practice of basic techniques. Sometimes a new skill is introduced after the basics. Basic technique practice might involve striking the air or moving together in the C step up and down the dojo floor. These step drills are an excellent practice for kata. Indeed, schools in which kata practice is limited often incorporate step drills with similar success.

It is during the dramatization experience, including kata and step drills, that the art of karate is nurtured. The sensei takes time to correct each student's technique, moving a hand here, a stance there. The result is that students come to appreciate and visualize the perfect technique. Step drills are followed by focus pad drills, one-step sparring, prearranged self-defense, and kata. Typically, sparring is the last activity. Many classes end with cool-down stretching, vigorous boot camp–style exercises, or meditation.

In developing a lesson plan or rank schedule, the sensei first considers the totality of expectations for first-degree black belt. A student must perform a number of kicks, punches, blocks, kata, one steps, self-defense drills, power or breaking using a focus pad or board, weapons, and supplemental arts (jiujitsu, escrima, kickboxing, etc.). Having written out the requirements for first dan, the sensei then divides the material into thirds. One-third will be taught to white, yellow, gold, and orange belt ranks (ranks 10 through 7); one-third will be taught only to intermediate ranks (6, 5, and 4); and one-third will be reserved for advanced students (ranks 3, 2, and 1).

AWARDING STUDENT RANK

Measuring level of improvement can be difficult, both for the sensei and the student. Awarding rank should be based on time in grade, knowledge of skills, demonstrated character traits, and skill performance. Sometimes it's difficult for students to understand or agree with the subjective evaluations of knowledge and character. When there's disagreement, the sensei should provide performance indicators that cannot be questioned.

For example, a yellow-belt student might demonstrate knowledge of basic kicks and the first kata. Convincing a beginner or his parents that his or her kata lacks focus based on a subjective evaluation is not definitive. Include performance evaluation requirements (e.g., the ability to kick at head level, performing 20 pushups in 20 seconds, accurately and forcefully striking focus pads, breaking a board, scoring points in sparring, etc.) that can be measured and understood by students and parents.

Dan Ranks

About six months after the student has earned the first grade of brown or red belt, he or she can test for first-degree black belt, or shodan. Many schools award a deputy, undecided, recommended, or shodan ho black belt for marginal students or good students who have a below average test. This rank requires a second exam to receive the full rank of first-degree black belt. During the three- to six-month waiting period, weaknesses can be corrected.

The first-degree black belt must demonstrate good character and a high degree of ability when performing kata, basics, one steps, and self-defense techniques. The first dan must be competent at different levels of sparring, including point and contact fighting. Here again, it's important to have easily measured, objective performance criteria that can be understood by all participants. At the dan level, a written paper should be required. Students must research a subject or answer questions prepared by the sensei. For example, the sensei might require students to answer questions or write a report about what they have learned by reading chapters one or two of this book.

Some schools permit only students who have earned a B-average in academic work to test for dan rank. Many schools require students to complete 60 to 100 hours of teaching lower ranks. The sensei prepares a list of all requirements for each rank level and makes these requirements available to students as they begin their study of karate.

The sensei must differentiate between junior and adult dan ranks. Adult rank begins at age 16. Juniors may earn dan rank; however, it should be understood that a junior might eventually forfeit dan rank if he or she does not test at age 16. Many schools require more time in grade for each level at junior rank. Some styles expand student grades from 10 to 14 to provide junior students ample time to mature at each rank.

When an adult earns the rank of first-degree black belt, he may become a sensei. It's advisable to have in place a teacher certification, usually acquired after completing a number of supervised or paid teaching hours. Properly taught students who are loyal to their sensei do not leave the dojo to become competitors with the sensei. High-quality schools are able to hire the new black belt or assist him or her in a franchise school at another location.

The dan ranks of first, second, and third are performance level ranks. Typically, the third dan is able to demonstrate the most athletic skills of all the dan ranks. The top competitors are often third dans. Note that black belts in their 30s and 40s are not expected to compete with younger black belts. This understanding applies in most organized sports. It's the rare student who at age 40 can compete well with an athlete of similar rank and 20 years younger. While time in grade may be the same for young and old, physical performance might vary. This same factor is present in the promotion of a 12-year-old black belt. Children may earn dan rank even though they are not expected to possess the physical prowess of adults.

To promote a student to first dan, the sensei must hold the level of at least second dan from a recognized organization. A first dan who has completed all of the requirements from a respected dojo has learned the bulk of information required to teach and promote through brown-belt level. All sensei should be a part of a regional or national organization at least until completing the level of fifth dan. Organization affiliation and support is especially useful to first- through fourth-degree black belts and can be used advantageously by all senior ranks.

Promotion from first- to second-degree black belt requires two years of hard training. Advancement to third dan requires an additional three years. Using this traditional scale, a second dan, if ranked as a first dan at the adult level at age 16, could achieve third dan at age 21.

Time in Grade

It takes much wisdom and maturity to achieve rank. The in-grade waiting period to advance from third to fourth dan is four years; from fourth to fifth dan, five years. Thus, the fifth dan would be awarded to experts who are at least 30 years old. Wisdom comes with age and experience. The fourth and fifth dan levels are teaching grades, signifying the title of master instructor. Black belts who earn dan rank and then retire, leave the dojo, fail to teach, or otherwise become inactive do not forfeit their dan rank; however, they must give up their time in grade.

A traditional system often mandates that the in-grade requirement for the next rank be equivalent to the desired rank. The period from fifth to sixth dan is six years; from sixth to seventh dan, seven years; and so on. Thus, the age requirements for rank eligibility are as follows: sixth dan, 36 years; seventh dan, 43 years; eighth dan, 51 years; and ninth dan, 60 years or older. The rank of 10th dan is reserved for senior masters who are 70 years or older. If all styles followed this system, there would be no concern about rank inflation. In a community of black belts, there would be very few 9th and 10th dans.

Merit

A merit system that awards the equivalent of time in grade for extraordinary accomplishments could add up to 10 years in grade equivalency. In other words, black belts may earn one to three years in grade for winning national or international championships. Publishing articles and/or books, producing instructional videos, and other work that advances the field also could earn one to three years of in-grade experience. Achieving national celebrity, which enhances the public perception of martial arts, can also earn one to three years of in-grade equivalency. And, of course, successful and productive teaching, the fundamental reason for advanced rank, earns in-grade experience. The merit system may be used to advance promotions by up to 10 years for most and perhaps 15 years for the select few extraordinary applicants for advanced rank. A world-title holder with significant publications, national celebrity, and a successful career of teaching individuals who have influenced the national or international practice of martial arts may legitimately carry the title of 10th dan in his or her mid-50s to early 60s.

For senior teaching and administrative ranks of fifth dan or higher, demonstrated physical skill is not a primary concern. One requirement for advanced rank is need. There must be a demonstrated need for awarding advanced rank. A fifth dan who is semi-retired from teaching and has a small club of beginning students does not demonstrate a need for higher rank. A fifth dan who is an active teacher and has several first, second, and third dan students does have a demonstrated need for advancement. A fifth dan who does not actively teach beginners but supervises one or more schools to assist in teaching and promotions also has a demonstrated need to advance in rank.

Some styles require that a master instructor have experience teaching students at least one dan rank below his or her current rank before advancing. Thus, a sixth dan must have taught and promoted one or more fifth dans before advancing to seventh dan. A grass-roots method used by some unaffiliated first dans requires that the first dan teach a student from the rank of 10th grade to first before advancing to second dan. The components of skill, age, need, and merit or recognition are worthy and necessary factors that must be considered when granting legitimate dan rank.

New Styles

In Japan and Okinawa, traditional masters often combined two or more styles to create new styles. These masters typically had decades of experience and senior dan rank as apprentices of nationally recognized systems. The practice of developing a new style has continued in the United States. The practice has become so popular that some styles are created even though there are no students or practitioners in the style.

There must be a demonstrated need to create a style. For a style of karate to exist beyond the imagination of the style's founder, there must be at least two generations of black belts in the new system. The founder teaches the new style of karate and develops a student of first-degree black belt within the new system. To withstand the test of time, the first dan must teach the founder's new system to the next generation, unaltered with no additions or deletions to the system. So long as the system produces new generations of black belts, it is in fact a new style and worthy of a name and recognition.

Becoming founder of a new style or system may merit a minor adjustment in dan rank advancement. The founder of the new style or system must be the highest rank within the system. Some mistakenly assume that the highest rank must be 10th dan or soke (a designation beyond rank). This is not true. The highest rank in the new system need only be the founder's current rank or a rank that is one degree higher than the most advanced student. All dan ranks for new styles should abide by the age requirements. The value of the new style is based not on the reputation of the founder but on the productivity of the new black belts developed within the system.

Titles

The title of master instructor typically is reserved for ranks of fourth dan and higher. Earning the title implies that the master is competent at teaching students of dan rank as well as other student grades. The master must have several generations of dan ranks in his or her lineage.

The title of grand master is awarded to those responsible for a significant number of master instructors. The grand master has achieved the rank of eighth dan or higher through a recognized system and in accordance with the age requirements. Just as a person cannot be a grandfather without having grown children who have produced a new generation, a karate grand master must have generations of students being taught by his or her master-level students. The legitimate title of grand master is quite rare.

False Titles

Perhaps because of perceived competition to recruit students from a limited regional market, titles have been created and falsified to lend an air of importance. A quick review of a large city's yellow-page ads reveals a significant number of grand masters, world champions, and "professors," all working in the same community. How do you know which sensei are impostors? Use the requirements outlined in this chapter and ask questions. Ask to observe a few classes. Talk to members of the class. Finally, try a few classes yourself. Don't be afraid to ask questions. The real masters are not intimidated and will want to answer all of your questions personally.

The desire for titles has resulted in a new unhealthy trend to lend the title of PhD to karate instructors. No accredited university in the United States or abroad recognizes or presents a PhD in martial arts. Earning a PhD requires four years of study at an institution to earn a bachelor's degree, another two years to earn a master's degree, and an additional two to three years of intense study to fulfill the requirements for the PhD, or doctorate. You must attend classes. You must take tests. You must conduct scientific research and defend that research before a board of professors. And you can expect to invest thousands of dollars in tuition, books, and living expenses during your years of full time study.

CONCLUSION

Modern American karate, still in its infancy, suffers from many problems, yet its probability for continued success greatly exceeds its potential for failure. Its greatest virtue is freedom of expression. What is of interest in one style or school might be viewed quite differently from the perspective of those in another style. There are many different interpretations of what works best in modern karate, and this is good. Competition continues to build a stronger martial art.

While it's natural and healthy for physical skills to vary, some commonality should exist within social skills. The pageantry and ritual, chain of command, ceremonial bow, and distinctive apparel (though it, too, varies) need to be enforced in part in all interpretations of karate. In recent years, modern karate schools have tended to move away from the limitations of style. Style now means a base art that is justifiably supplemented with other arts that are effective. I hope that the trend toward creating unnecessary titles, often used to lure unsuspecting students, disappears over time.

A major theme of this book has been the concept of change. A need for change led to the freedom to develop and promote new skills. The price for freedom was the realization that the teachings of old-school karate were in some ways deficient. They could not produce self-defense, open competition, or mixed martial arts skills with the same efficiency and reliability as reality-oriented modern American systems. But some Americans who for years bowed diligently to old-school superiority shed their association with the Asian arts

For the diligent student of karate, success may be measured through personal satisfaction or external awards.

too quickly. If they had been misled to believe that the physical skills were superior, perhaps the total concept of traditional karate would prove inappropriate for American students as well. In their haste, some American instructors, including Asian Americans, who spent many years carefully learning the traditional training methods, were ready to attempt to replace the social patterns as well.

It's difficult to believe in pageantry and ritual and adhere to a chain of command if it is based on less than sound concepts. Karate was marketed in the United States as a physical skill, not as a means of developing social skills, such as discipline, honor, respect, humility, trust, and loyalty. The Asian martial arts are quite successful in the development of social skills. They are less successful in quickly developing self-defense skills. As the credibility of martial arts wavered through the abandonment of the beliefs in the physical superiority, the social structure was often abandoned as well. This has proven to be a mistake that should be corrected.

My research has led me to believe that both traditional and modern karate should concern both character development and the acquisition of physical skills. In this regard, the traditional masters were right. I fully believe the art of the empty hand would have continued quite well without American intervention.

Still, we should recognize that through technological and ideological advances, Americans have developed training methods that are more functional as both self-defense and sport systems than some of the Oriental methods. Americans have not, however, improved on the old-school social structure (except, perhaps, to add a positive upbeat attitude to the discipline). The wise and prudent martial artist still seeks to combine modern karate skills with an adjusted military social structure (while allowing for relative differences in cultural backgrounds). Future research in martial arts education should be directed toward ascertaining information concerning specific ramifications of this approach.

The way to mastery can be attained through different paths. Each holds value. Identify your own path somewhere between the ultra-traditional styles and the contemporary eclectic systems. Maintain your desire through a change of habit and your discipline through dedication. When you are older, you will have at last achieved mastery. Until that time, we are all to remain as students in search of a master.

Peace.

BIBLIOGRAPHY

Unpublished Research

Jerry Beasley, "Contemporary Karate: An Examination of the Social Relations and Group Configurations in a Modern Day Adaptation of the Ancient Oriental Martial Art." (EdD dissertation, Virginia Polytechnic Institute and State University, 1980)

Jerry Beasley, "The American Sensei: A Sociological Study of the Occupational Role of Karate Instructor." (master's thesis, Virginia Polytechnic Institute and State University, 1977)

R. Stull, "Measuring Speed in the Karate Punch." (paper presented at Karate College, 1990)

Books

Corcoran, J. and E. Farkas. *The Complete Martial Arts Catalogue*. New York: Simon and Shuster, 1977.

De Vos, G. *Socialization for Achievement*. Berkeley: University of California Press, 1973.

Draeger, D. and R. Smith. *Asian Fighting Arts*. Tokyo: Kodansha International Limited, 1969.

Eliade, M. *Rites and Symbols of Initiation*. New York: Harper Torch Books, 1958.

Funakoshi, G. *Karate-Do: My Way of Life*. New York: Kodansha International Ltd., 1975.

Goffman, E. *The Presentation of Self in Everyday Life*. New York: Doubleday Anchor Books, 1959.

Haines, B. *Karate's History and Traditions* (revised edition). Boston: Charles E. Tuttle Company, 1995.

Haislet, E. *Boxing*. Greenville, North Carolina: Bemjo Martial Arts Library, 1982.

Kaplan, A. *The Conduct of Inquiry*. San Francisco: Chandler Publishers, 1964.

Manheim, S., and Simon, B. *Sociological Research: Philosophy and Methods*. New York: Homewood, Inc., The Dorsey Press, 1977.

Nicol, C. *Moving Zen: Karate As a Way to Gentleness*. New York: Dell Publishing Co., Inc., 1975.

Rielly, R. *The History of American Karate*. Jersey City, NJ: Semper Fi Co., Inc., 1976.

Smith, H. *Strategies of Social Research*. Newark, NJ: Prentice-Hall, 1975.

Urban, P. *The Karate Dojo*. Boston: Charles E. Tuttle Co., 1967.

Periodicals

Beasley, J. "A Foundation in Formlessness: A New Look at JKD." *Karate Illustrated* 10 (March 2000).

Beasley, J. "To Float in Totality: The Philosophy of Jeet Kune Do." *Martial Arts Legends* (March 2000).

Beasley, J. "A New Look at the Old Concept of Range." *Black Belt* (November 1999).

Beasley, J. "Finding Liberation from Classical Karate: A Fresh Look at Bruce Lee's Classical Treatise." *Black Belt* (September 1999).

Beasley, J. "Classical Kata: The Fine Art of Fighting an Opponent Who Isn't There." *Black Belt* (April 1999).

Beasley, J. " Martial Artist, Liberate Yourself." *Black Belt* (April 1999).

Beasley, J. "Is Trapboxing the Ultimate Fighting Art?" *Karate/Kung Fu Illustrated* 28: 22 (December 1997).

Beasley, J. "Sport Karate's Tremendous Trio: Reminiscing with Three Karate Pioneers." *Black Belt Yearbook* 33: 20-24 (July 1997).

Beasley, J. "Jeet Kune Do's Contributions to American Independent Karate: Is Today's Full-Contact Karate Actually an Extension of JKD?" *Karate International* 7: 41-42 (October 1996).

Beasley, J. "The Myth of the Ultimate Martial Art." *American Karate* (September 1989).

Beasley, J. and James Herndon. "Ranks, Titles and Claims of Grandeur." *Karate International* (July 1989).

Beasley, J. "The JKD Matrix." *Inside Kung Fu* (April 1989).

Beasley, J. and Joe Lewis. "Strategy." *Karate International* (March 1989).

Beasley, J. and Joe Lewis. "Beyond Angular Attack." *Black Belt* (June 1988).

Beasley, J. "The Development of American Ninjutsu." *Black Belt* (January 1986).

Beasley, J. "Preventing Injuries During Stretching Exercises." *Karate Digest* (March 1985).

Beasley, J. "How to Become a Superkicker." *Karate Digest* (Spring 1984).

Beasley, J. "American Karate: A Pursuit of Freedom." *Kick Illustrated* (December 1981).

Beasley, J. "The Development of American Karate." *Karate Illustrated* 10 (October 1979).

Beasley, J. "How important is an instructor's image?" *Karate Illustrated* 9 (December 1978).

Congalton, A. "Medical Students Predictions of Public Opinion Regarding Role Performance of Doctors." *Journal of Vocational Behavior* 1 (Spring 1971).

Corbett, J. "Martial Arts Spas: The Future Arrives." *Black Belt* 17 (October 1979).

Corcoran, J. "The Untold Story of American Karate." *Black Belt* 15 (August 1977).

Kenyon, G. "Sociological Consideration." *Journal of the American Association of Health, Physical Education and Research* 39: 31-33 (November-December 1968).

Lee, B. "Liberate Yourself from Classical Karate." *Black Belt* (September 1971).

McGee, J. "Why We Study Karate." *Official Karate* 10 (July 1974).

McPherson, D. "Socialization and Sport Involvement." *Encyclopedia of Physical Education* 5 (1978).

Nishioka, Y. "Making Men in Karate." *Black Belt* 10 (October 1972).

Stevenson, C. "Socialization Effects of Participation in Sport: A Critical Review of the Research." *Research Quarterly* 46: 287-301 (October 1975).

Volsky, M. "How Dojo Practice Can Improve Relationships." *Black Belt* 10 (October 1980).

Weinberg, S. and H. Aron. "The Occupational Culture of the Boxer." *American Journal of Sociology* 57 (Spring 1957).

Young, R. "JKD and the Professor: An Interview with Dr. Jerry Beasley, Jeet Kune Do's Premier Researcher." *Black Belt/Bruce Lee* (March 2001).

INDEX

Note: Photos and illustrations have italicized page numbers. Tables are indicated by an italicized *t*.

ABOUT THE AUTHOR

Voted the first Instructor of the Year for the 21st century and inducted into the *Black Belt* magazine's Hall of Fame, Dr. Jerry Beasley received the martial arts world's highest distinction. *Inside Karate* magazine called him "the published authority on American karate." *Black Belt* magazine recognized him as America's foremost martial arts educator. Dr. Beasley was the first American to earn both a master's degree (1977) and doctorate (1980) in part for his research in martial arts teaching and curriculum design from Virginia Tech, Blacksburg, Virginia. Beasley first gained attention in 1973 when he decisioned then ITF world champion, Ho Kwon Kang of Venezuela, in an exhibition bout. A multiple dan holder in moo duk kwan, karate, taekwondo, hapkido, tang soo do, and jiujitsu, and a certified instructor of jeet kune do, Dr. Beasley was the first person to earn the 8th dan (1995) from his mentor, world champion Joe Lewis. The certificate was authorized and cosigned by Bill "Superfoot" Wallace. He was awarded the 9th dan in 1999 from Professor Wally Jay and Grand Master Michael De Pasquale Sr.

In 1998, Dr. Beasley received the Distinguished Alumni Award from Virginia Tech's department of sociology. A professor at Radford University, he is a three-time recipient of the College of Education and Human Development's Outstanding Scholarly Activity Award. He holds a U.S. patent for the invention of the Flash inter-vehicular communication device, an innovation in highway self-defense. With a martial arts career spanning five decades, Dr. Beasley is known as the dean of America's collegiate martial arts professors. He can be reached through the Web site **www.aikia.net.**